THE ARAB WORLD
AFTER DESERT STORM

MUHAMMAD FAOUR

UNITED STATES INSTITUTE OF PEACE PRESS
WASHINGTON, D.C.

United States Institute of Peace
1550 M Street, N.W.
Washington, D.C. 20005

©1993 by the Endowment of the United States Institute of Peace

First published 1993

Printed in the United States of America

The paper used in this publication meets the minimum requirements of American National Standard for Information Sciences—Permanence of Paper for Printed Library Materials, ANSI Z39.48-1984.

Library of Congress Cataloging-in-Publication Data
Faour, Muhammad, 1952–
    The Arab world after Desert Storm / Muhammad Faour.
        p.   cm.
    Includes bibliographical references and index.
    ISBN 1-878379-30-5 (alk. paper) : $15.95 — ISBN 1-878379-31-3 (pbk. : alk. paper) : $24.95
    1. Arab countries—Politics and government—1945- I. Title
DS63.1.F34 1993
909'.09749270829—dc20   93-29014
                                                                 CIP

To my late father, Hajj Ali Faour,
who made the education of his children
the mission of his life

Contents

Foreword

လၢၣ Ask an American or a European what the Gulf War accomplished and the reply is likely to be along the lines of "Evicted Iraq from Kuwait," with perhaps some further reflection on the destruction of Iraq's military might or the rejuvenation of the Middle East peace process. Ask an Arab and the reply is likely to be very different and almost certainly much longer.

For the Arab world, the Iraqi invasion of Kuwait and the subsequent defeat of Iraq by the U.S.-led coalition have had complex and sometimes profound effects. Virtually all aspects of Arab life have been touched to some extent: politics and economics, demography and ideology, interregional and extraregional relations, religious tension and ethnic strife.

Trying to sort out these effects and decide which are evanescent and which enduring is an exceedingly difficult task, especially with the Gulf War only two and a half years distant. Muhammad Faour, however, has risen to the challenge. As the reader will discover, the author has combined diligent research with thoughtful analysis to produce a book that is both exceptionally informative and provocative. Drawing on his own experience as well as a broad range of Arabic and English-language sources, Faour examines the changes that have occurred since the end of the Gulf War and speculates on the changes that are likely to occur in the coming three to five years. Not all of these developments necessarily result from the Gulf War, since a number of them were in train well before the war began. The picture he presents, though it contains both light and dark, is in essence a bleak and unsettling portrait of the present and future of the Arab world.

Operation Desert Storm emerges from this book as the equivalent of an enormous earthquake that has rearranged various features of the Arab landscape, and the aftershocks of which are rumbling still throughout the region. Political structures that tottered before the war—such as the largely ineffective system of regional cooperation—have collapsed or been all but abandoned, while old disputes have been brought again to the surface. Similarly, vulnerable ideological constructs—pan-Arabism is the preeminent example—have finally fallen apart. And even the more robust elements of the Arab world—the economies of the rich Gulf states, for instance—have been shaken.

At the same time, however, other prominent features of the Arab landscape seem to have escaped more or less intact. The essential authoritarianism of most Arab regimes has not given way to demands for democracy (a somewhat ironic strand of continuity given the predictions of many Western observers on the post–Gulf War future for Arab democracy). Popular disaffection too is unabated; indeed, it may have increased. Unless regimes commit themselves to democratization, warns Faour, political instability seems certain to worsen, with militant Islamic movements spearheading the forces of dissent.

Focusing on six key Arab states—Algeria, Egypt, Iraq, Jordan, Kuwait, and Saudi Arabia—the author brings out the differences among countries and subregions as well as showing the similarities among them. As noted above, Faour's diagnosis of the Arab world as a whole is not encouraging, although he finds some reason for guarded optimism at least as far as the Israeli-Arab dispute is concerned. By pointing up the current divisions among Arab states and the military limitations of even the best-armed of them, and by accentuating the destabilizing social, economic, and political forces at play across the region, he argues that the Gulf War has made the continuation of the present status quo more dangerous for the Arabs than a potential negotiated settlement with Israel. Hence, the peace talks begun in Madrid in September 1991 have continued despite the kind of political events that probably would have halted previous attempts at such dialogue.

This book represents the outcome of research undertaken while the author was a Peace Fellow in the Jennings Randolph fellowship program of the United States Institute of Peace. As is true for all Jennings Randolph fellows, Muhammad Faour's views are, of course, his own. They are derived from the totality of his experience in analyzing the Middle East, not merely from the research he conducted on the effects of the Gulf War. His commitment to informed and open debate about the causes and consequences of conflict is one which the Institute shares wholeheartedly, even though it does not take a position on the opinions he expresses. The Institute was created by Congress to strengthen the nation's capacity to promote the peaceful resolution of international conflict. We believe that this timely, informative, and stimulating study of one of the world's most strife-torn regions is a valuable contribution to that effort.

Charles E. Nelson, Acting President
United States Institute of Peace

Acknowledgments

This book began as a research proposal on the impact of the 1990 Gulf crisis on the Arab world. By offering me a Peace Fellow award in 1991–92, the Jennings Randolph fellowship program of the United States Institute of Peace gave me the opportunity to carry out this research in a friendly, intellectually stimulating atmosphere. Many thanks go to the board of directors of the United States Institute of Peace, its former president Samuel Lewis, and its current acting president, Charles Nelson. Special thanks are due to the staff of the Jennings Randolph fellowship program— Michael Lund, the director of the program, Otto Koester and Joseph Klaits, the program officers, and Barbara Cullicott, the program administrator—for their technical assistance, moral support, and friendliness.

I am particularly grateful to Joseph Klaits for his useful comments during the preparation of the manuscript and his continuous encouragement, and to Barbara Cullicott, whose continuous, sincere help was exemplary. Assigned to me were two research assistants: Tarak Barkawi during the first few months, and Paula Bailey-Smith until the end of my fellowship term. Both deserve special thanks for the various tasks they performed.

Several ideas in this book have stemmed from discussions and interviews with a number of scholars, journalists, and politicians from the United States and the Middle East; their names are listed in the Sources Used section of this book. They all deserve my deep gratitude. Although some of my ideas and views may not be similar or even close to those of any particular name listed, each of them helped me, perhaps unknowingly, in defining some concepts and/or polishing others. I also owe thanks to four anonymous external reviewers of the first draft for their useful comments and overall positive attitudes. I tried to incorporate most of their suggestions in the final draft.

I am more than grateful to Nigel Quinney, a former editor at the United States Institute of Peace, who followed the development of the manuscript from its crude outline to the present form. Not only did he help in clarifying vague ideas and editing every chapter, but he saw to it that the manuscript went to publication at the earliest possible time.

Finally, I am very grateful to my wife Basma and our two wonderful children Jana and Samer, all of whom showed high tolerance for the long hours I spent away from home and continued to shower me with their sincere support and love.

The Arab World After Desert Storm

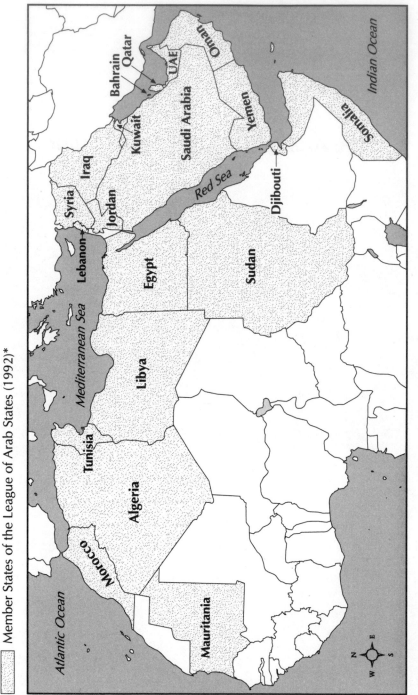

Member States of the League of Arab States (1992)*

*Palestine is considered by the League an independent state and therefore a full member.

one

Introduction

The Gulf War, which began with Iraq's incursion into Kuwait and ended in the humiliating defeat of Iraq at the hands of the U.S.-led world coalition, constitutes an important watershed in the recent history of the Middle East. This event, which precipitated a global crisis, is pivotal for several reasons. First, Iraq's aggression was unprecedented. Never before in the twentieth century had one Arab state occupied and subsequently annexed another. Second, the Gulf War was the first regional war fought against an Arab state by a coalition of Western and Arab countries with Israel's blessings. Egyptian, Saudi Arabian, and Syrian assertiveness even extended to the point of a public condemnation of Iraq's launching of Scud missiles against Israeli cities; one Arab regime had never condemned another for attacking Israel.

Third, for the first time in the twentieth century, non-Muslim, Western military forces launched an offensive against an Arab country from Saudi Arabia, the land of the two most sacred shrines of Islam. Despite the legitimation of the offensive by some Muslim religious authorities, other Muslim clergy and activists considered the Saudi act blasphemous. Fourth, unlike previous wars, this war produced a popular reaction that was neither uniform across the Arab world, nor consistent from the beginning to the end of the crisis. For example, in Arab states that allowed people to express their feelings freely, demonstrators supporting Iraq marched in the streets, while in the states that participated in the Gulf War, popular reaction was closer to passivity. Some influential Islamic groups that opposed Saddam Hussein in August 1990 later became his staunch supporters.

3

Clearly, the Gulf War has left deep scars that will continue to have a profound effect on Arab society and politics for years to come. Specific questions about the nature of these scars, however, and their implications for peace, security, and stability in the Middle East remain. These questions may be addressed by examining the social and political changes that have taken place since the Gulf War and by speculating about the changes that are likely to occur in the coming three to five years in a number of Arab states.

The diverse, long-term effects of a significant historical event like the Gulf War will take many years to completely disentangle and fully comprehend. Even at the time of this writing—January 1993— not enough time has elapsed to permit an unclouded and definitive view of the effects of the Gulf War. Yet, it is by no means impossible or unhelpful to look now for signs of far-reaching changes in the Arab world that the Gulf War either engendered, accelerated, or redirected. Nor is it fruitless to seek evidence of continuity: Although the Gulf War may have produced surprising changes, it also seems to have had far less effect on certain aspects of Arab politics and society than many observers, especially in the West, predicted. An investigation of both the continuities and the changes is the purpose of this study.

Placing this analysis in its proper historical context requires an overview of Arab politics and society. The remainder of this chapter first offers a brief sketch of the Arab world and then outlines a number of issues affecting various Arab countries, from the Levant to the Maghreb to the Gulf. No special emphasis is given to any particular country or subregion, as such details appear in subsequent chapters. Rather, the purpose is to show how the entire Arab world has been affected by global trends, especially those arising from the end of the Cold War.

ARAB POLITICS AND SOCIETY: A BACKGROUND

Today, the Arab world extends from the Arabian/Persian[1] Gulf on the east to the Atlantic Ocean on the west, a vast area that exceeds 4.6 million square miles and embraces 20 states, with a combined population of about 235 million.[2] A sense of identification with a single "Arab nation" is "firmly in place both as a collective self-perception" by Arab citizens and "as an identification rubric used by outsiders."[3] In spite of the diverse definitions of the term "Arab," all Middle Eastern scholars agree that the common denominator among residents of the Arab world is their language. Formal Arabic is an official language in all countries of the Arab League. In addition to their common language, most Arabs share the same religion. The overwhelming majority (over 90 percent) are Muslims, predominantly of the Sunni persuasion, and Islam is a vital force in everyday life.

Despite its linguistic, religious, and cultural cohesion, the Arab region is rich in diversity. In territorial size, some countries (Sudan and Saudi Arabia) comprise vast areas that approach 1 million square miles while others (Bahrain) are small enough to fit into a major Western city. The population size ranges from 500,000 for the tiny city-states of the Gulf (Bahrain and Qatar) to 26 million in Algeria, Morocco, and the Sudan, and up to 55 million in Egypt; however, half the Arab states have populations of under 5 million. Economically, a wide disparity exists between the rich oil states, with per capita incomes ranging from $5,000 (Libya) to $20,000 (United Arab Emirates), and the poor, labor-exporting countries, where per capita incomes are under $1,300 (Jordan) and can be as low as $100 (Somalia).[4] The combined indigenous population of the "upper-income" countries[5] falls well under 10 percent of the total population of the Arab world.

Great disparities also exist in education. Several Arab countries have high rates of illiteracy; 52 percent in Egypt, the most populous country, and up to 76 percent in Somalia. By contrast, the majority of adults in several states (such as Kuwait, Lebanon, and Jordan) are literate, and a large number hold college degrees. Substantial differences also exist among Arab states with respect to infant mortality, average family size, and ethnic and sectarian composition.[6]

Although most Arabs are Sunni Muslims, Shi'i Muslims make up a majority in Iraq and form large communities in Lebanon, Bahrain, Kuwait, and Saudi Arabia. Syria is ruled by the 'Alawis, who emerged as a dissident branch of Shi'ism. The Druze, another offshoot sect of Shi'is, form a cohesive, influential community in Lebanon and Syria. Christian Arabs also constitute significant proportions of citizens in individual states. In addition, there are small numbers of other minority religious groups such as Jews and Baha'is. The ethnic composition of the Arab world is also diverse, including not only Arabs but also a few million Kurds in Iraq and Syria, a significant percentage of Berbers in Morocco and Algeria,[7] a large community of Armenians in Lebanon and Syria, and a large number of non-Arab Africans in the Sudan.

One way to capture this diversity is to divide the Arab world territorially into four areas that have, to a large extent, distinctive historical and sociocultural features.[8] The first of these is the Arabian Peninsula, which includes Saudi Arabia, five small Gulf states, and Yemen. Inhabitants of the peninsula speak similar Arabic dialects and have similar dress codes and social mores. All have maintained a Bedouin heritage, and some of their tribes share common ancestors. Conservative, puritan Islam is the prevailing political culture. The Arabian Peninsula has proved to be the area least hospitable to pan-Arabism and least cooperative with other parts of the Arab Middle East.[9]

The second area is the Nile Valley (Egypt and Sudan, particularly the northern part), which shares the same Arabic dialect, African connection, water resources, borders, and historical experience, including Egypt's occupation of Sudanese territory. Egypt, the cradle of many ancient civilizations, had the characteristics of a sovereign nation long before the modern concept of a nation began to crystallize.

The Fertile Crescent or Arab Levant (Jordan, Iraq, Syria, Lebanon, and the Palestinian population) is a third area in which a number of ancient civilizations took root. Levantines share similar social values, dialects, dress codes, urbanity, and drive for education. These states are most prone to pan-Arabism and extreme political ideologies.[10]

The Maghreb (Morocco, Algeria, Libya, and Tunisia) people share similar dialects that are hard for other Arabs to understand. The colonial legacy, particularly that of the French, is a distinctive feature of this area.

The social stratification system in the Arab region is complex, with both domestic and intercountry dimensions. Each society is stratified in terms of religion, ethnicity, socioeconomics (income, education, and occupation), residence, and background. Status is defined also by an individual's tribe or clan (its power and influence, size, and relation by descent to Prophet Muhammad) and family within the clan. Enormous social differences exist between countries based on the availability of natural resources and human resources, the quality of life, the religious and sectarian composition, the ethnic composition (Arab and non-Arab), and prestige and historical legitimacy of rulers or ruling families.

THE ARAB WORLD IN THE POST–COLD WAR ERA

The end of the Cold War made it possible for the United States to forge a world coalition against Saddam Hussein and to win the Gulf War with negligible losses.[11] Well before the outbreak of the

Gulf crisis, however, some features of the new international system began to have a significant impact on Arab politics and society, most notably the demise of the Soviet Union as a superpower; the resultant transformation of the role of the United States in world leadership; the international trend toward economic and political liberalization; and the revival of national, ethnic, and religious identities.

U.S.-Led Multipolarism

With the dissolution of the Soviet Union, the United States has become the world's sole political and military superpower, a development that has had a profound impact on the Middle East. Perhaps the most immediately apparent results of this transformation are that cooperation has replaced competition in the resolution of the Arab-Israeli conflict[12] and that new restrictions have been imposed on transfers of weapons of mass destruction.

Although America's commitment to Israel has remained firm, Israel's strategic importance to the United States is said by many observers to have declined.[13] At the same time, Arab allies of the former Soviet Union, whether they be governments or political or paramilitary groups, cannot turn to its Russian successor for protection or support if they pursue radical policies or engage in military adventures. Commitments made by the former Soviet leadership to Arab allies, including bilateral defense or cooperation treaties, have been either scrapped or greatly restricted. Sensing their vulnerability, many of the former Soviet clients in the region have turned to the United States.

The cutback of arms transfers by the new Russian government has led many Arab states to seek other suppliers, such as China and North Korea. Although sufficient to safeguard the Arab states' national security, Chinese and Korean weapons are limited in diversity and quality (perhaps with the exception of the Scud C missiles available to Syria). By contrast, the security concerns of the United States' Arab allies—notably Saudi Arabia, Kuwait, and Egypt—are met with a continuous flow of sophisticated U.S. weapons such as fighter planes, tanks, and missiles. The end of the Cold War has resulted in severe international restrictions on the transfer of technology for weapons of mass destruction, such as nuclear bombs and chemical and biological weapons, thereby limiting the ambitions of some Arab regimes—notably Iraq and Syria—to attain strategic parity with Israel, which has nuclear technology.

The changes brought about by the end of the Cold War are not limited to the political and military spheres. Although the United States remains the world's largest economic power, the emergence of Japan and the newly integrated Western Europe as major economic players has led rich Arab states to start expanding their economic ties beyond the United States. Meanwhile, the economic woes of poorer Arab regimes threaten their political stability. While the United States can provide much help, either bilaterally or through international financial agencies, assistance from the European Community and Japan could ultimately reorient the policies of these Arab governments.

Economic Liberalization and Democratization

Since the late 1980s, political liberalization has swept over various parts of the globe. Although the end of the Cold War was not the sole inspiration, the fall of Soviet Communism has certainly accelerated, fortified, and broadened the process of political liberalization. In a dramatic shift, which the noted American political scientist Samuel Huntington calls "global democratic revolution," many countries have switched from authoritarianism to some form of democracy.[14]

During the past two decades, transitions from nondemocratic to democratic forms of government have far exceeded reverse transitions. Regimes that have democratized began their transformations from a variety of authoritarian forms: dictatorship, military regime, oligarchy, or single-party regime. The processes of democratization, and the results, have been diverse. Some states have adopted two-party systems, others multiparty systems or parliamentary democracies, and still others have adopted presidential systems. But common to almost all transitions has been "selection of a government through an open, competitive, fully participatory, fairly administered election."[15]

Concomitant with democratization is a powerful trend toward economic liberalization. The failure of centralized, planned economies—as demonstrated in the former Soviet Union and in Eastern Europe—was not the only factor in the process. Nondemocratic regimes have been pressured both by their domestic constituencies and by international monetary organizations (mainly the World Bank and the International Monetary Fund) to bring their economies in line with the prevailing international order. The drive toward economic privatization is gaining increasing momentum in regimes that are democratizing as well as in nondemocratic political systems. It seems that autocratic governments are recognizing the need for a transition to a market economy. This change, however, can generate popular demands for political liberalization, which may, ultimately, lead to democracy. In fact, many analysts, especially in the United States, believe that a market economy is a necessary condition for stable democracy.[16]

The international trend toward democratization and market economy has important implications. First, the concept of democracy is strongly associated with freedom and liberty, which are widely cherished values. Second, many scholars contend that democratic states do not tend to engage in violent conflicts with one another.[17] If this view is correct (and it should be noted that it is still the subject of much debate), as more countries democratize so the world will become more peaceful, and it is possible that democracy in the non-industrialized countries will, in the long run, produce prosperity.[18]

These powerful international trends had a visible impact on the pre–Gulf War Arab world, where authoritarianism and socialist economies were creating popular dissatisfaction. The demand for liberalization was expressed in a variety of forms. Street demonstrations and social unrest in several countries often followed hikes in the prices of food and other basic commodities implemented under reforms mandated by the International Monetary Fund. Petitions to rulers, articles in newspapers and magazines, and informal meetings between prodemocracy activists and Arab governments all featured demands for some opening of political systems and the transformation of economies toward the market system.

The response of Arab governments was generally accommodating, at least superficially. Between January 1988 and July 1990, national elections to legislative bodies were held in the then–Yemen Arab Republic, Jordan, Iraq, Syria, and Kuwait. Municipal and provincial elections took place in Algeria. Egypt held national elections in the midst of the Gulf crisis in November 1990. Several formerly socialist states decided to privatize their economies. The extent and pace of transformation varied, however, from one country to another. For example, economic change was limited and slow in Iraq, Algeria, and Syria but kept a moderate pace in Egypt.

Revival of Ethnic and Religious Aspirations

The breakup of the former Soviet Union into independent states and the demise of socialism in Eastern Europe have facilitated the expression of deep-rooted ethnic beliefs and religious feelings that had been suppressed for decades. For example, Serbs, Bosnians, and Croats have demonstrated their conflicting national aspirations in Yugoslavia, while Muslims in Azerbaijan and other central Asian states have sought to assert their religious identity. There has also been a surge of long-suppressed feelings of transnational group identity, such as that of the Kurds in Iraq, Iran, and Turkey. The resultant social unrest and bloody domestic conflicts are expected to continue as ethnic or religious minorities seek to govern themselves within states that often show little respect for their rights.

The revival of ethnic and religious aspirations frequently breeds radical political movements as an "antithesis" to prevailing suppressive regimes. Such movements may be racist or religious fundamentalist in nature. The latter are perhaps particularly dangerous, for when political extremism is clad in religious garb it can acquire a sacred character in the eyes of its supporters, emboldening them to refuse compromise and to challenge the status quo by force. Instability and bloody civil wars are too often the result.

A variety of Islamic groups with conservative, liberal, and radical orientations have emerged or have reactivated, seeking a political role. Their messages appear to have been well received by large numbers of young Muslim Arabs whose problems have not been addressed, nor basic human needs satisfied, by their regimes. After witnessing the failure of existing ideologies and regimes to provide them with food, services, and jobs while repressing them often ruthlessly, the young Arabs seem to have found refuge in Islam.

The religious renaissance has not been limited to Islam. Among Israeli Jews, fundamentalist groups have become increasingly active. Christian Arabs have also begun to demonstrate their religious distinction and loyalty more visibly. For example, in Egypt and Jordan, many Christians have started to observe religious rituals more regularly and to celebrate their holidays with greater fanfare. This resurgence of religious feelings has occurred, at least in part, as a reaction to the rise of Islamic radicalism and increasing demands on the part of many Muslims for the application of Islamic law (*shari'a*) in Arab societies that have a Muslim majority.

Palestinians have long been struggling to assert their distinctive national identity. While upholding, at least in theory, the concept of pan-Arab nationalism, the Palestinian guerrilla movement and the Palestine Liberation Organization (PLO) have emphasized the independence of the Palestinians from all other Arabs. The call for Palestinian self-determination, the demand for an independent state, the independence of the PLO from all other Arab regimes, and the severing of relations between Jordan and the West Bank all testify to the strongly held national aspirations of the Palestinians.

ORGANIZATION AND METHODOLOGY OF THIS BOOK

Each of the following chapters focuses on a different aspect of the Arab world after Desert Storm. Chapter 2 examines the Gulf War's demographic and economic impact, especially in those countries that have experienced the most severe effects. The enormity of the economic and human costs of the war is perhaps little appreciated outside of the Middle East. The aim of this chapter is to convey, if not the exact costs of the Gulf crisis, then certainly a good sense of the scale of economic dislocation and human displacement and suffering.

Chapter 3 discusses trends toward political liberalization in Arab countries, beginning in the pre–Gulf War era. In the immediate aftermath of the war, the Western media speculated that the trend toward political liberalization and democratization sweeping various regions of the world would eventually reach the Arab countries, particularly those that were directly involved in the war. This chapter searches for signs of a significant move in that direction by surveying changes in political systems, state bureaucracies, militaries, ruling parties, opposition groups, and political ideologies.

Chapter 4 analyzes the decline of pan-Arabism in the face of territorial nationalism and the rise of political Islam, ideological changes that were accelerated by the Gulf crisis, although their roots lie in events of the preceding two decades. Inter-Arab relations and the new Arab order, or disorder, are studied in chapter 5. Chapter 6 takes a close look at the implications of the sociopolitical changes described in earlier chapters with respect to the Arab-Israeli conflict and prospects for stability and peace in the Middle East.

This book is an investigation of specific topics from a comparative, cross-country perspective. Selection of the topics was based partly on the author's interest and area of expertise but chiefly on his judgment of the importance of the changes taking place in the subject examined. Since a detailed study of all 20 members of the Arab League would be a work of several volumes, this book examines only those Arab states that have manifested significant social and political changes. Other states are referred to when they demonstrate the nature of the change their neighbors may undergo in the future.

Six countries—Iraq, Kuwait, Saudi Arabia, Egypt, Jordan, and Algeria—are singled out for examination. Not all six feature prominently in each chapter, however; rather, attention is centered on those countries in which topic-relevant changes have occurred. For example, in Iraq, Kuwait, and Saudi Arabia no popular Islamic movements that warrant special examination have emerged in the wake of Desert Storm, whereas Egypt, Jordan, and Algeria have witnessed a rising influence of Islamic fundamentalism. (*Fundamentalism* is used in this book to denote the restrictive interpretation of Islam that demands strict adherence to the letter of the *shari'a*; *Islamist* is used to refer to all groups—including, but by no means restricted to, the fundamentalists—seeking greater state recognition of Islamic culture, traditions, tenets, and interests.)

Each of the selected cases has a special significance. Iraq, a major Arab power in the Fertile Crescent whose oil reserves are second only to those of Saudi Arabia, created a global crisis by occupying Kuwait. Kuwait, whose rich resources and strategic location motivated the international coalition's efforts, was the victim of Iraq's aggression. Saudi Arabia, a regional power and the leader of the Arab Gulf states, is a pillar of the world economy whose stability and security is of vital strategic interest to various international parties. It is also the site of the two most sacred mosques of Islam, visited by millions of pilgrims each year. Egypt represents the Nile Valley group of Arab countries. It is the most populous Arab state and the only one to have established peaceful relations with Israel, which it has maintained for over a decade. The long-established self-confidence that was demonstrated by this step, along with Egypt's Western support, were crucial to its leadership of the Arab coalition against Saddam Hussein. Jordan was the only pro-Western neighbor of Iraq that did not join the anti-Saddam alliance. It has also played a central role in the Arab-Israeli conflict because of its location and large Palestinian population. Algeria is a major Maghreb state that, until recently, played a leading role in the Third World and in the nonaligned movement. Algerian Islamic fundamentalists were denied a virtually assured popular mandate by the cancellation of runoff elections in January 1992. Together, the six selected countries account for over half the total Arab population and for about 47 percent of the world's proven oil reserves.[19]

Despite their political, economic, and military importance in the region and in the world at large, the six selected countries do not manifest all of the social and political complexities of the entire Arab world; nor are they statistically representative of all Arab countries, despite belonging to the four distinct territorial areas described earlier. However, the comparative study of several well-selected cases can produce important knowledge about the nature and extent of change in the phenomena investigated. Without doubt, a comparative analysis provides a better, broader vision of issues than does a single case study.

As of January 1993, two and one-half years have elapsed since Iraq invaded Kuwait. This book assesses the impact of the Gulf War by comparing today's situation in the Arab world with the situation before August 2, 1990. It takes into account significant changes that have occurred since the independence of the selected countries as well as detailing the course of key political, economic, and social developments between August 1990 and January 1993.

The research for this book drew chiefly on two types of sources. The first source is published literature in English and Arabic, including scholarly material from fields such as political science, international relations, demography, and sociology, as well as journalistic works. In addition, journals of various kinds and many Arabic, American, and European magazines and daily newspapers were monitored from September 1, 1991, through January 15, 1993. The second source of data is personal interviews with a host of experts on the given countries. These experts include academics, journalists, writers, public officials, and politicians from the Middle East and the United States. (Complete lists of published materials used and people interviewed are provided in the Sources Used section toward the end of this book.)

Inevitably, the diversity of sources yields a diversity of facts, figures, and opinions. Rather than merely describing this variation, this book seeks to indicate what seem to be the most reliable of reports, the most plausible of statistical estimates, and the most popularly held opinions. For instance, the approach in chapter 2, which analyzes the economic and demographic consequences of the Gulf crisis, is to report the range of most recent values given by diverse sources, each with an unknown and probably wide margin of error. Within each range, a single value ("a point estimate," as statisticians call it) usually is offered that seems to this author the most plausible gauge of the extent of change in the relevant demographic and economic areas. The aim is not to compute a number of statistics with maximum precision, but rather to highlight major changes and powerful trends that even approximate, conservative estimates such as these will illuminate. Likewise, in those chapters dealing with the internal politics of the Arab nations and the nature of the Arab regional system, the actions and opinions of a wide variety of political actors are not only described but also evaluated in the light of past experiences, current developments, and likely future scenarios.

This approach is, of course, inherently judgmental. In seeking to present a balanced portrait of the Arab world after Desert Storm, the author has drawn on his own knowledge and experience in assessing the reliability and accuracy of the numerous sources of information used in the course of this study. No doubt some readers will take issue with the author's characterization of particular Arab regimes, with his assessment of the most probable outcome of a government's present policy, or with his understanding of an opposition group's current strategy. Such a critical reading is welcomed. Hopes for peace and stability in the Arab world will be advanced not by the persistence of misconception, ignorance, or silence, but by the widening and deepening of informed debate and open-minded dialogue.

two

Demographic and
Economic Changes

ℰℰ The Gulf War, the subsequent suppression of opposition
forces in Iraq, and the expulsion of Palestinians and
Bedoons from Kuwait caused significant demographic and economic changes across the Arab world. Although many Arab countries were affected, the changes were felt most acutely in six—Iraq,
Kuwait, Jordan, Saudi Arabia, Yemen, and Egypt. This chapter on the
demographic and economic changes wrought by the Gulf War will
focus on those six countries, examining the experience of each in
order to paint a picture that is at once wide-ranging and detailed.
The impact of the war on Yemen will be dealt with under the
section on Saudi Arabia, since the latter's expulsion of Yemenis was
the major consequence of the war for Yemen.

As this chapter illustrates, the Gulf War and its aftermath have
caused much more economic and demographic upheaval in the
Arab world than is generally recognized. The costs of the war, even
to many of those countries on the side of the victorious U.S.-led
coalition, have been enormous. The financial burdens of the war
have been extremely heavy, straining even the richest Arab nations
and causing substantial distress to their poorer neighbors. Probably
upwards of 100,000 people died as a result of Desert Storm and the
Iraqi suppression of the Kurds and Shiites. Perhaps more shocking
is the scale of social and demographic dislocation following Desert
Storm; millions in the Arab world—including not only Kurds and
Shiites, but also Palestinians, Bedoons, Yemenis, Egyptians, Sudanese,

and others—have become refugees or have been forced to leave the countries they inhabited before August 1990.

Quantifying the costs of the Gulf War is not a straightforward task. Due to the haphazard nature of information registration systems in most Arab countries, particularly in relation to population, relevant data are often scarce and, when available, rather inaccurate. Therefore, the approach taken by this study is to report the most recent estimates given by diverse sources and then to suggest which of those seems the most plausible. Of course, given the limitations of the data, complete accuracy is impossible. Fortunately, however, the statistics are sufficient for the main purpose of this chapter, namely, to highlight the major changes and powerful trends affecting the post–Gulf War Arab world.[1]

IRAQ

Demographic Changes

Two years after the end of the long, devastating war with Iran, Iraq initiated another Gulf War, thereby bringing about an even greater disaster for itself, for Kuwait, and for other parties as well. In 43 days, thousands of Iraqi soldiers and civilians were killed in the air raids. The total number of Iraqi war casualties is a subject of debate, as neither the U.S. government nor the Iraq government has shown interest in compiling these data or in releasing the limited data available. Thus, estimates of the total death toll of Iraqis vary from 10,000 to 100,000.[2] Reuters reported on March 4, 1991, that 85,030 Iraqis were killed in action. U.S. military officials put the toll at 75,000 to 105,000.[3] Daponte, a demographer at the U.S. Census Bureau, computed 40,000 military and 13,000 civilian deaths.[4]

Although we may never have an accurate count of Iraqi deaths, in the words of the U.S. secretary of defense, there is no doubt that the second Gulf War, the subsequent domestic rebellions, and the economic sanctions together claimed as many casualties as the first Gulf War. In addition to the 53,000 killed in military operations, Daponte calculated 35,000 deaths in domestic upheavals and 70,000 others due to lack of medicines and poor sanitation, resulting in a total of 158,000 casualties.[5] According to *Middle East Report*, by May 1991, at least 8,000 Iraqis had been killed in northern and southern Iraq as a result of domestic fighting, and an additional 20,000 Kurds, mostly children, died from disease and harsh environmental conditions. This calculation brings the total number of Iraqi deaths to well over 100,000.[6] By comparsion, according to conservative Western estimates, the Iraqi death toll in the eight-year Iran-Iraq war totaled 105,000.[7]

The war had other serious demographic consequences beyond direct military casualties. Mortality and migration levels were considerably altered, while deaths caused by waterborne and airborne diseases rose because of a combination of factors: scarcity of essential medicines such as vaccines and antibiotics (insulin and anti-cancer drugs were also in short supply); food shortages and malnutrition; lack of potable water; and poor sanitary conditions. Infants and children were most vulnerable, followed by the elderly and the handicapped. According to an 87-member team from Harvard University, which assessed health, nutrition, and other socioeconomic conditions in Iraq in the summer of 1991, infants (i.e., children less than 12 months old) experienced a 3.5-fold increase in mortality from 23 to 80 deaths per 1,000 live births. Equally dramatic was the increase in mortality among children under five years of age, from 28 to 104 deaths per 1,000 live births. Approximately 900,000 children—29 percent of those surveyed—were found to be malnourished. Of these, 118,000 were at risk of death due to malnutrition.[8] The Iraqi minister of health reported that, during the first four months of 1992, upwards of 40,000 people died as a result of the economic embargo, of whom some 15,000 were children under age five.[9] Although this figure may be exaggerated given the vested interest of its source, there is reason to believe that many people died during (and after) this period for health reasons related not to political suppression but to the effects of wartime destruction inflicted by the coalition forces and sanctions authorized by the United Nations.

The Gulf crisis and the subsequent military operations in January and February 1991 forced most resident expatriates to flee Iraq. The Egyptians were the largest group of foreigners to repatriate. Most of the 800,000 Egyptian farmers and skilled workers returned home, along with thousands of other Arabs, mainly from Jordan and Lebanon. The next largest group of fleeing foreigners, estimated at more than 100,000, were from the Indian subcontinent: Bangladeshis, Pakistanis, Indians, and Sri Lankans. Between August 2, 1990, and late February 1991, a total of approximately 1 million foreigners left Iraq.[10] During March and April 1991, the volume of population movement among Iraqis rose dramatically. Surprisingly, the vanquished Saddam quickly reorganized the remnants of his armed forces and managed to crush the domestic revolts that flared up in both northern and southern Iraq. Anticipating massive killings and atrocities by Saddam's army, nearly 1.8 million Iraqis, mostly Kurds, fled to Turkey and Iran. The majority of these refugees headed toward Iran, which slowly permitted them, along with tens of thousands of Shiite Arabs from southern Iraq, to enter its territory. By early May 1991, some 1.4 million Iraqis had taken refuge in Iran, while another 400,000 had fled to Turkey.[11]

Several thousand refugees died of starvation and disease before the United Nations took the unprecedented step of establishing a security zone in northern Iraq, the objective of which was to provide a safe haven for at least 850,000 Kurds stranded in the freezing mountains along the Iraq-Turkey border. Under the protection of UN forces, hundreds of thousands of these people were able to return to their homes. However, thousands of houses in the security zone had been partially or completely destroyed in the Kurdish uprising against the Iraqi regime. Subsequent Iraqi attacks forced thousands of Kurds to flee their homes and made it unsafe for others to return.[12] UN agencies, along with some nongovernmental organizations (NGOs), launched a massive international relief operation and managed to address the most urgent needs of refugees and returnees for shelter, food, and health. Yet, by the end of 1992, some 3 million inhabitants of "Free Kurdistan" remained short of food, fuel, and other basic needs under a tight economic blockade enforced by the Iraqi army.

Shiites, who revolted unsuccessfully against the regime, were forced to flee from their homes in southern villages and cities in apprehension of brutal retaliation by Saddam's army. Several thousand of them are presently living in the southern marshlands (Aghwar), where the Iraqi army has difficulty tracking them down. By enforcing a "no-fly zone" below the 32nd parallel in which only coalition aircraft are permitted, the United Nations has protected the Shiite rebels from Iraqi air raids. These rebels and their families, however, have no direct access to the food rations distributed by the government, the United Nations, and other relief organizations.

Another group of refugees fled to Saudi Arabia, which granted refugee status to them as well as to thousands of former prisoners of war. As of January 1992, some 35,000 Iraqis, predominantly Shiites, were living in two camps—Rafha and Artawya—close to the Saudi-Iraqi border under the watchful eyes of Saudi security forces.[13] Their movement was restricted, and they were not allowed to work, but the Saudis provided them with food and other basic essentials at no charge. Others have sought refuge in Iran, which estimated the number of Iraqi refugees within its borders in late January 1992 at 100,000.[14] This number is unlikely to have dropped by January 1993, in view of the dire economic conditions and political suppression that continue under Saddam's rule.

Economic Changes

Iraq's economy suffered gravely from both the military operations and the economic sanctions. The coalition forces inflicted massive damage on the country's infrastructure, reducing it to a "preindustrial" state, according to a UN commission that visited Iraq immediately after the war. Western sources estimate that about 80 percent of Iraq's infrastructure was destroyed or badly damaged.[15] As much as 90 percent of electricity facilities, oil refineries, and industrial establishments were destroyed.[16] According to a UN report, the coalition's forces succeeded in destroying all of Iraq's modern communications systems, along with 35 of its approximately 90 bridges.[17] Although available assessments may be incomplete or inaccurate, conservative estimates of the damage to buildings, roads, bridges, communications, power plants, oil installations, and other forms of infrastructure point to a minimum cost of $50 billion.[18] Other estimates of the cost of reconstruction go as high as $150 billion.[19] In addition, Iraq lost at least $40 billion in military equipment.[20]

The most serious economic loss was in oil revenues, which before the war accounted for virtually all of the country's export earnings. About half of Iraq's forecasted oil revenues for 1990 ($7.7 billion)[21] were lost in addition to at least 95 percent of its revenues between January 1991 and August 1992. Despite the continuation of economic sanctions against the Iraqi government, which remains adamantly opposed to the United Nations' proposed sale of $1.6 billion worth of its oil,[22] truckloads of oil have crossed to Jordan, Iran, and Turkey almost daily. The Kurds have exported a small quantity (between 2,000 and 10,000 barrels a day) of crude oil to Turkey and Iran, apparently with the implicit approval of UN guards.[23] Revenues from smuggled oil are unknown, but given the stringent sanctions against oil exports, Iraq's oil revenues still would have declined by at least 95 percent. Based on a constant price of $16 per barrel and its 1989 daily export of 2.8 million barrels, Iraq would have earned upwards of $27 billion. Thus, by August 1992 the total of lost oil revenue may be conservatively estimated at $35 billion.

Although heavily indebted, the Iraqi economy must also absorb the costs of repatriating victims of its government's aggression and costs of UN missions. According to Western estimates, claims for damages will range from $50 to $100 billion, to be paid by a percentage levy on Iraqi oil revenues. The United Nations established a special compensation fund in Geneva for victims, including both individuals and governments. Iraq appealed for a five-year grace period, revealing that its outstanding debt at the end of 1990 totaled $43.32 billion, an interest due of $32.35 billion, and $30 to $40 billion in so-called "grants" from other Gulf states. Debt service for 1992 will require $34.24 billion, and the total for the period 1991–95 will amount to $75.45 billion.[24] Thus, at the end of 1992, the total amount of debt, "grants," interest, and debt service exceeds $107 billion, while the total economic cost of the Gulf War, including infrastructure damage, loss of military hardware and oil revenues, and war compensation payments, is conservatively estimated at no less than $175 billion.

Nevertheless, by late 1992 Iraq had made remarkable progress in repairing war damage, despite the acute embargo-imposed shortage of construction materials and spare parts. Accurate independent estimates of the costs of restoring damaged infrastructure are unavailable, but all independent reports agree that the extent of reconstruction so far has been impressive, particularly in the oil sector, and that the economy has coped well despite increasing personal hardship.[25] According to the Iraqi government, 75 percent of the damage to industrial projects had been repaired by the end of February 1992, although not all of the projects were operational. By July 1992, most bridges were functioning, and electric power was near normal at 90 percent of prewar capacity. As of May 1992, the danger of malnutrition in Iraq ceased to exist, according to the World Food Programme.[26] In addition to UN and NGO food rations distributed to the needy, the government provides every citizen with a ration of basic staples at reduced prices.

KUWAIT

Demographic Changes

No accurate figures exist on Kuwaiti war casualties, but experts interviewed by Middle East Watch agree that most of the deaths resulted from the Iraqi occupation rather than from the military operations of August 2, 1990. The Iraqi government crushed both peaceful and armed Kuwaiti resistance with utmost brutality. According to Middle East Watch, scores of civilian Kuwaitis were summarily executed in detention centers and in public while their families and neighbors watched in horror. Some of the executed were merely suspected of peaceful opposition to the occupation. The total number of people killed by Iraqi forces by mid-October 1990 is estimated at 1,000, including 600 Kuwaitis.[27] Of those Kuwaitis, over 120 had been killed for engaging in nonviolent resistance. Scores of Kuwaiti nationals and residents are believed to be detained in Iraq, a claim which the Iraqi government has repeatedly denied. However, the number of these supposed prisoners of war is declining as missing persons are either found to be living abroad or confirmed dead. In April 1992 the Kuwaiti government reduced its estimate of their number from an often-cited figure of 2,000 to 850.[28]

In the months immediately following the liberation of Kuwait, particularly March and April 1991, many more people died—this time at Kuwaiti hands. A government-inspired campaign against those suspected of collaborating with the Iraqi occupiers led to extrajudicial summary executions and deaths in detention caused by torture and/or inadequate medical care. Again, no firm figures are available.[29] Senior government officials condemned abuses but acknowledged that some killings had taken place, blaming "vigilante elements." However, none of those "elements" was charged or brought to trial. According to Middle East Watch, scores of expatriates were killed by Kuwaiti forces, including 54 unidentified individuals discovered in mass graves. A majority of the identified victims were of Palestinian or Iraqi origin.[30]

The executions and tortures perpetrated by the Iraqi forces during occupation and by government-inspired armed Kuwaitis after the liberation were heinous crimes that violated the most basic of human rights. Yet, the death toll of the war and its aftermath in Kuwait has little demographic significance in comparison with that of Iraq or of other Arab countries during times of civil unrest or wars with Israel. The mass displacement of "undesirable" groups, particularly Palestinians, was of far more demographic consequence for Kuwait. These groups include nationals of countries that did not support Desert Storm—notably, Jordan, Yemen, and the Sudan—in addition to Palestinians, resident Iraqis, and stateless Arabs (Bedoons).

At the time of the Iraqi invasion, the population of Kuwait totaled approximately 2.2 million, nearly 750,000 of whom were Kuwaiti citizens. Palestinians, numbering between 300,000 and 400,000, composed the single largest foreign community in Kuwait and the wealthiest Palestinian community in the Arab world. Most of them held Jordanian passports, but thousands were stateless, with roots in Kuwait that went back many years. The first substantial Palestinian migration took place in the wake of the creation of the Jewish state in 1948. A second wave came in the late 1950s when Kuwait exempted Palestinians and Jordanians from visas, and a third in 1967 after the Israeli occupation of the West Bank. Possessed of a variety of skills as well as higher levels of education than Kuwaiti nationals and other Arabs, Palestinian immigrants assumed influential positions in the government bureaucracy, in educational institutions, and in private companies. A number of thriving business enterprises were headed and staffed by Palestinians.

Until the Iraqi invasion, Palestinians were generally on good terms with the government, although events in the Middle East occasionally created tensions between the PLO and the Kuwaiti leadership, whose concerns regarding state security and regime stability were heightened during the Iran-Iraq war. The ruling family apparently was becoming increasingly uncomfortable, however, with the long-term presence of a powerful, cohesive minority that was deeply entrenched in various segments of Kuwaiti society. This discomfort was exacerbated by the presence of thousands of stateless Palestinian refugees to whom neither Israel nor any Arab country would offer citizenship. Herein lie the roots of the Kuwaiti hostility toward the Palestinian community, a hostility that surfaced dramatically during the Gulf crisis and was exacerbated by the PLO's support of Saddam Hussein and Palestinian collaboration with the occupiers.[31]

When Kuwait was liberated, there was an indiscriminate backlash against all Palestinians, collaborators or not. Despite instances of support for the resistance and many heroic efforts to save Kuwaiti lives and property, the Palestinians were rejected as a community of traitors.[32] In the words of Ibrahim al-Shatti, *chef de cabinet* of the Emir:

> The Jordanians and the Palestinians are treacherous peoples. They betrayed the hospitality and generosity shown them. They lived off the wealth of Kuwait and the Kuwaiti people. . . . The problem lies with the Palestinian people, who have no loyalty, unlike for example the Lebanese, Syrian and Egyptian peoples. The latter live for a few years as migrants (in Kuwait) and then return to their own countries. As for the Palestinians, when they left Palestine, it dropped out of their memory and they forgot it.[33]

The government expelled most of the Palestinians and other "undesirables" from the emirate, using a variety of methods—both constitutional and unconstitutional. Expatriates who left the country were barred from returning. Even in cases where they held valid residence permits, they were required to apply for readmission, which was not granted to unwanted national groups. All foreigners who left the country and returned during the occupation were considered illegal residents subject to deportation. The Ministry of the Interior was authorized to deport, without obtaining a court order, any foreigner who committed a serious traffic offense. The contracts of all foreign employees of the government were terminated retroactive to August 2, 1990. All residence permits in Kuwait were required to be reissued by October 1991.[34] This deadline was subsequently extended a few times.[35] The process required affidavits from Kuwaiti sponsors (i.e., employers) certifying that the applicant did not collaborate with the Iraqi occupation. Any form of cooperation with the Iraqis, such as attending work or school during the occupation, was considered collaboration.[36]

During the Iraqi occupation, the population of Kuwait dropped to about 700,000, including some 200,000 Palestinians. After liberation, the Palestinians, Bedoons, Iraqis, Sudanese, and most of the Egyptians who left were not permitted to return. The government placed additional pressure on the remaining Palestinians, actually deporting some of them. According to the U.S. State Department, a total of approximately 5,700 foreigners were deported by May 1992.[37] By mid-January 1992, the Palestinian community in Kuwait had been reduced to under 50,000[38] and by July 1992 to under 40,000.[39] Kuwaiti officials plan to reduce that number to 10,000 or 15,000, a goal that is likely to be achieved early in 1993, given the little-publicized but steady migration of Palestinians from Kuwait.

The next largest group of unwanted expatriates are the Bedoons, who before the war numbered approximately 250,000.[40] The Bedoons are Arabs of no specific nationality who have resided in Kuwait for most of their lives. The majority were born in Kuwait of Syrian, Saudi, or Iraqi origin, and strove in vain for years to become permanent residents. The government claims that many of them are nationals of other states who have hidden or destroyed their identity papers in order to justify their overstay. It therefore considers all Bedoons foreigners. They are generally underprivileged, living in slums with little access to social services. Before the war, they were principally employed as rank-and-file members of either the armed forces or the police force, which provided them with important welfare benefits.

By mid-January 1992, the number of Bedoons had been reduced to under 100,000[41] and may continue to drop, though at a much slower rate than that of the Palestinians. By September 1991, some 8,000 Bedoons who had been denied admission into Kuwait were stranded in Iraq and at a camp on the Iraq-Kuwait border.[42] The Saudi daily *Asharq al-Awsat* reported that over 5,000 of these exiled Bedoons were married to Kuwaiti women. Neither these men nor their children were permitted to return to Kuwait, and some influential Kuwaitis (including former members of the now defunct National Council) contend that Kuwaiti women who marry foreigners should be required to emigrate to their husbands' native countries.[43]

Economic Changes

The Gulf War had an unprecedented economic impact on Kuwait. According to the Pentagon, Kuwait paid its pledged financial support to Operation Desert Storm, a total of $16 billion, in full. Damage to buildings, roads, and other infrastructure is estimated at $20 to $25 billion,[44] only $3 billion of which applies to damage done to oil facilities. Loss of oil revenues caused by the five-month interruption of production in 1990 amounts to about $4.93 billion.[45] For 1991, estimated oil revenues fell short of the level expected in 1990 by $10 billion, and in 1992 the revenues were short by about $5 billion.[46] Thus, the total loss in oil revenues as a result of nonproduction reached $20 billion at the end of 1992. In addition, an estimated 6 million barrels of oil a day were lost as a result of the burning of oil wells.[47] In the nine months required to extinguish the fires, losses totaled approximately $20 billion, while fire-fighting operations consumed nearly $1.5 billion.[48]

In all, war-related costs amount to no less than $83 billion. However, calculations of the total economic loss must also include the cost of restoring the environment—both in Kuwait and in the Gulf region in general—to its prewar status. Of particular concern are the large quantities of oil spilled into the ocean and desert, both of which were caused by Iraqi attacks on oil wells.

The social and political consequences of the Gulf War have also had a profound effect on the Kuwaiti economy. For example, government efforts to reduce the number of foreigners residing in Kuwait have shrunk the population by nearly half. A survey conducted in

May 1992 reported a total of 48,631 vacant apartments in the emirate, nearly 40 percent of the total number of residential apartments.[49] Prewar rents in the capital dropped by 50 percent, and once-thriving quarters of Kuwait city turned into "ghost towns, with shuttered stores and empty streets."[50] In addition, the general quality and quantity of service available in both the public and the private sectors has deteriorated because of the loss of highly qualified workers, particularly Palestinians. Until those expatriates are replaced, which may take some time, Kuwait's economy is not likely to return to its prewar vigor and growth.

The surge in government spending is another example of the interdependence of sociopolitical and economic factors in the aftermath of the war. Apart from the cost of reconstruction and rehabilitation, compensation of war victims, end-of-service payments for terminated employees, and the shared financial burden of Operation Desert Storm, the budget for the 1991/92 fiscal year included a huge increase in defense spending and a significant increase in social insurance allocation. In comparison with the 1990/91 budget, the after-war budget of $31.3 billion increased the percentage allocation for defense spending from 12 to 43 percent. Social insurance was allocated almost double its share in the earlier budget because of the substantial increases in child allowances and welfare payments to citizens.[51]

Furthermore, in an effort to win the support of business enterprises, the Kuwaiti cabinet and later the National Council approved the allocation of $20 billion to bail out local banks, which had incurred bad loans since the early 1980s.[52] Some of these banks are said to be owned by members of the ruling family. In addition, in May 1992, the government decided to write off citizens' utility bills to the state and proposed to buy hundreds of vacant apartments, thereby increasing its spending by several hundred million dollars.[53]

Increased expenditures notwithstanding, the steady increase in oil production has translated into a steady increase in state revenues, and continued rapid growth is projected for the coming years (assuming regional stability). While the current account for 1992 was in deficit by $2 billion (one of the highest figures in Kuwait's history), the 1993 account is forecast to produce a surplus of $5 billion.[54] Thus, thanks to Kuwait's vast oil reserves and the sophistication and small size of its indigenous population, the Kuwaiti economy will eventually be restored to its prewar vigor.

JORDAN

Demographic Changes

Although Jordan was neither the site of battles nor an active party to the conflict, the impact of the Gulf War on Jordan was exceeded only by its effects on Iraq and Kuwait. The nature of its economy, the composition of its population, and its geopolitical status, made Jordan particularly vulnerable; it is a small country with few natural resources, a large population of Palestinians, and neighbors who are much stronger and potentially expansionist. Prior to August 2, 1990, Iraq was not only a much stronger Arab neighbor, but also Jordan's principal trading partner.

Jordanian demographics were decisively altered by the Gulf crisis. Although Palestinians may have accounted for less than half of the total population before the war,[55] they now constitute a majority. An estimated prewar Palestinian population of 3 million[56] increased by nearly 10 percent in the wake of the Iraqi invasion of Kuwait, as Jordanian nationals, resident in Kuwait for decades, streamed into the country. They had lost their jobs or businesses and were forced to abandon their life savings and most personal belongings. When the war ended, the Kuwaiti government would not permit these evacuees to return to the country.

Economic Changes

Prior to the Gulf War, the Jordanian economy was in poor condition, suffering from a decline in remittances and a large foreign debt. The influx of the Palestinians and the increase in political tension with the Arab Gulf states imposed further hardships. According to the International Monetary Fund (IMF), the balance-of-payments current account for 1989 showed a deficit of $82 million, which widened to $754 million in 1990.[57] Overall, the economic and financial loss to Jordan as of the summer of 1991 was estimated by Ibrahim Oweiss, an economist at Georgetown University, at $2 billion. Other estimates put the loss as high as $5 billion.[58]

The disruption of sea traffic to 'Aqaba between August 1990 and May 1992 is estimated to have cost the Jordanian economy $46 million,[59] and the government has also lost $400 million in annual remittances sent by Jordanians previously employed in Kuwait.[60] Unemployment, which by October 1991 had increased to about 30 percent nationwide, has remained at that level,[61] with refugees suffering a much higher rate of 83 percent.[62] In addition, a sense of betrayal arising from Jordan's stance toward the coalition forces caused the Arab Gulf states—principally Saudi Arabia and Kuwait—to suspend $500 million in annual aid.[63]

As Iraq was Jordan's principal prewar trading partner, purchasing at least 23 percent of its exports and supplying it with over 80 percent of its petroleum requirements at a reduced price, the outbreak of the war and the subsequent enforcement of UN economic sanctions against the Iraqis has had a profound impact on the Jordanian economy. In August 1990, Saudi Arabia pledged to supply half of Jordan's petroleum needs, in the form of free shipments worth $1 million per day.[64] Jordan's reluctance to comply with UN sanctions, however, soon led the Saudis to suspend all oil supplies.[65] As a result, the Jordanians became even more dependent on sharply limited supplies of Iraqi oil, which, until mid-January 1991, were trucked into the country.

Despite the resumption of export activity with Saudi Arabia and other Gulf countries, the economy of Jordan remains in straitened circumstances. The budget deficit made up 18 percent of the gross domestic product (GDP) in 1991. According to the governor of the Central Bank of Jordan, foreign debt stood at $7.2 billion as of February 1992. Nearly $600 million is also required to service this debt each year. In 1992, remittances dropped to $614 million and foreign aid to $475 million.[66] Although the government has been complying with IMF demands to reduce the budget deficit (for example, by raising subsidized fuel prices), the deficit for 1992 reached $745 million.[67] Nevertheless, the general economic outlook for 1993 is more positive. The economy is undergoing structural change that promotes efficiency in the public sector and less state control in the agricultural and industrial sectors, where the private sector is leading. This reform in state policy coincides with the return from Kuwait of experienced, energetic Palestinians, some with considerable capital.[68] Jordan's debts with the Paris and London Clubs were rescheduled, and there are signs of economic growth, which is projected to reach 3 percent in real GDP growth in 1993. The current accounts deficit is expected to fall steadily until the middle of the 1990s, assuming no new regional crises occur.[69]

SAUDI ARABIA

Demographic Changes

Saudi Arabia retaliated against Yemen's neutral stance in the Gulf War by withdrawing the special privileges enjoyed by some 1.5

million Yemenis in the kingdom. As of September 1990, all Yemeni expatriates were required to have Saudi sponsors (i.e., employers). Unable to satisfy this new condition, most Yemenis had to return to their home country. By November 1990, 700,000 had left, and many others were set to depart.[70] The number of those remaining in the kingdom has not been revealed by the Saudi authorities,[71] but the fact that about a million work visas were issued to Egyptians in 1991[72]—presumably to replace the departing Yemenis—suggests that close to a million Yemenis were expelled. Nationals of other Arab states that did not support Operation Desert Storm have generally been allowed to stay.

In the wake of the union between the former Yemen Arab Republic and the Popular Democratic Republic of Yemen, the outflow of Yemeni refugees from Saudi Arabia, combined with the 45,000 Yemenis who returned from Iraq and Kuwait,[73] has had profound political and economic consequences. The forced migration has increased the level of political tension between Yemen and Saudi Arabia, initially sparked by the Gulf crisis; it also has placed a heavy economic burden on Yemen, which is the poorest and least developed country in the Arabian Peninsula and among the three least developed members of the Arab League. By April 1991, Yemen had lost some $1.5 billion in remittance earnings,[74] a figure that was likely to treble in the following 18 months.

Economic Changes

The economy of Saudi Arabia was less affected by the Gulf War than were the economies of Kuwait and Iraq. Indeed, oil price increases in the wake of the invasion of Kuwait resulted in an oil revenue windfall of about $13 billion. But Saudi economic losses far outweighed gains. Early in 1991, Saudi officials estimated their total economic losses as a result of the Gulf crisis at $51 billion, excluding expenses such as oil spill clean-up, maintenance of the thousands of refugees who fled Iraq following their unsuccessful revolt against Saddam, and contributions to Turkey, Egypt, and Syria.[75] Based on Saudi official sources, one scholar estimated that in 1990 the kingdom paid some $30 billion to cover the cost of new weapons, loan commitments to the former Soviet Union and other countries, the cost of sudden increase in oil production, and other war-related expenditures. In 1991, the Gulf War bill reached an estimated $34 billion, thereby raising the total expenses related to the war to $64 billion.[76] This estimate is close to that of the U.S.

State Department, which put the total cost of the war to the Saudis at $60 billion, and to that of the leading Saudi daily, *Asharq al-Awsat*, which estimated $65 billion.[77] The total cost includes a $16.84 billion contribution to Operation Desert Storm[78] and $4.8 billion in aid to non-Gulf countries that suffered as a result of the Gulf crisis.[79]

The 1992 budget of $48.3 billion increased spending by 27 percent over 1990 levels, with a substantial percentage of the budget (30 percent) earmarked for defense spending. Borrowings from local and foreign banks totaled $8 billion. No budget was produced for 1991. Instead, government spending was based on the 1990 budget. During 1990 and 1991, Saudi Arabia overspent by some $50 billion, a figure that may approximate—though it probably falls short of—the cost of the war during this period.[80]

Despite the fact that 1992 marks the seventh year of deficit spending, in March 1992 the Saudi cabinet announced reductions in the prices of gasoline and cooking gas, and in telephone, water, and electricity charges. These reductions, which range from 28 to 68 percent,[81] were designed to improve the living standards of lower-income people, which had declined precipitously in the aftermath of the Gulf War. Such measures strongly suggest that the Saudi government sees the need to employ economic incentives to maintain its legitimacy and to foster social stability, even if such measures delay recovery. Nevertheless, given Saudi Arabia's immense oil reserves, the conclusion of Operation Desert Storm should enable the government to maintain a manageable current accounts deficit, which is projected to decline from an estimated $5.7 billion in 1992 to $4.7 billion in 1993.[82]

EGYPT

Demographic and Economic Changes

The Gulf crisis had an immediate impact on the Egyptian economy. The portion of the budget allotted to security increased, while exports declined. Earnings from the Suez Canal fell by $0.5 billion, and the tourist industry lost some $1.25 billion. Most of the million or so Egyptians resident in Iraq and Kuwait returned home during the war, costing the government approximately $2 billion per year. One scholar estimated the total economic cost of the Gulf War to Egypt at $3.5 billion,[83] and the country was left with an estimated budget deficit of $2 billion.

At the same time, however, Egypt was generously rewarded for its effective role in rallying Arab support for the coalition war against Iraqi aggression. In fulfillment of its pledge to aid countries adversely affected by the Gulf crisis, Saudi Arabia provided Egypt with a $1.79 billion emergency aid package,[84] part of which was designated to help relocate Egyptian evacuees from the Gulf region. It also issued nearly a million work permits to Egyptian workers, thereby replacing the Yemenis expelled from the kingdom. Kuwait and Japan also made emergency donations. The Saudis wrote off $4 billion in outstanding Egyptian loans, and the United States consented to write off $7 billion in debts for arms purchases. Other countries followed suit, resulting in the decline of Egypt's foreign debt from nearly $50 billion to $36 billion by early 1991. In May 1991, the Paris Club decided to write off $10 billion of the $20 billion Egyptian debt over a three-year period and to reschedule payment of the remaining $10 billion.[85]

Thus, on balance, the Egyptian economy appears to have gained—and is enjoying steady growth—as a result of the Gulf War. In December 1991, Egypt won IMF approval for its overall performance. Foreign exchange reserves surpassed the target level, and the exchange rate was unified ahead of schedule. Public sector reform, which emphasizes privatization and restructuring, has continued, albeit at a slower pace than required by the World Bank.[86] The number of Egyptians working abroad has returned to its prewar size of 2.5 million, and the amount of remittances sent back to Egypt has risen accordingly.[87] Nevertheless, Egypt continues to face economic difficulties; the budget deficit remains high, despite the government's success in reducing it to 7 percent of the GDP in 1991–92 and its efforts to reduce it to a target value of 5 percent of GDP in 1992–93.[88] Further cuts in government subsidies are planned, and more price increases and taxes are expected.[89] Although these measures may lead to a long-term improvement in economic performance, in the short term they generate higher unemployment. By mid-May 1992, unemployment in Egypt had reached 20 percent of the estimated 14 million in the work force, and it is expected to continue its upward trend for some time.[90]

A HEAVY BLOW

This chapter has revealed the depth of the impact of the Gulf War on the demography and economies of Iraq, Kuwait, Jordan, Saudi Arabia, and Yemen. Irrespective of the degree of accuracy of available statistics, even the lower bounds of conservative estimates illustrate the tremendous demographic and economic consequences of this war. Over 5 million civilians were forced to move from their places of residence to safer places within the same country or to other Arab or non-Arab countries. In Iraq, approximately 2.8 million people experienced involuntary migration, a fate shared by nearly half that number in Kuwait and close to a million in Saudi Arabia. Probably upwards of 100,000 Iraqis died as a result of war operations and the insanitary conditions and medical insufficiencies that prevailed in its wake, and thousands more continue to suffer from malnutrition and disease.

Of the demographic changes in the wake of the war, the most relevant to Arab politics and society are the displacement of (1) some 350,000 Palestinians from Kuwait mainly to Jordan, (2) close to a million Yemenis from Saudi Arabia, and (3) nearly 1.8 million Iraqis, mostly Kurds, within their country. These massive, involuntary movements of population are likely to sow the seeds of dissension, hostility, and revenge within and between Arab countries.

The economy of Iraq has been devastated, with economic losses set to exceed $175 billion by the end of 1992 and a total debt (with interest and service charges) of no less than $107 billion. Kuwait's economy was dealt a heavy blow; losses of more than $83 billion do not include the cost of environmental rehabilitation and compensation of war victims. Saudi Arabia's cost will top $60 billion, and Jordan's already strained economy was burdened with an extra $2 billion. To be sure, the rich Arab countries of the Gulf are no longer as rich as they were on the eve of the Iraqi invasion, and the poor Arab countries (except Egypt) have generally grown poorer. The economic gap between the "haves" and the "have-nots" of the Arab world remains wide.

The demographic and economic changes that have occurred in the Arab world in the wake of the Gulf War have diverse and complex sociopolitical implications. Their complexity stems, in part, from the interrelationship of demography, economics, politics, and society. The following three chapters investigate the relationship between economics and demography, on the one hand, and political liberalization, ideological changes, and inter-Arab relations, on the other. The concluding chapter relates the findings from this and the other chapters to the Arab-Israeli conflict and to the prospects for peace and stability in the Middle East.

three

Democratization or Modernizing Authoritarianism?

のの The military and political outcome of the Gulf War has led some Western journalists, scholars, and policymakers to expect an accelerated transition to democracy in the Arab countries, even the dynastic states of the Gulf. They believe that the political liberalization and democratization sweeping various regions of the world constitute a powerful international trend that will be reinforced by the military victory of democracies in the Gulf. Other writers, however, have a different assessment. They foresee a decelerated, impeded democratic transition caused by the heightened security fears of the Arab regimes, particularly in the Gulf.[1]

In reviewing the current status of democracy in six Arab countries, this chapter[2] finds little support for the optimists' position. Arab democracy seems to be largely a new facade on an old system of authoritarianism. Some ambiguous signs of movement toward greater democratization can be detected, but they in no way suggest a speedy or irreversible shift away from authoritarianism. The Gulf War may have increased popular demands for democracy and elicited from reluctant Arab regimes some prodemocratic rhetoric, but it has not significantly reduced the obstacles to democratic development posed by the nature of state and political leadership and the prevailing social structure and political culture in the Arab world. Little evidence suggests that the enlarged role the United States now plays in the region will offer real advantages to Arab prodemocracy forces; on the contrary, despite the best intentions of some members of the U.S. policy establishment, the enhanced U.S.

presence may actually bolster the power of the existing oligarchies and dictatorships, at least in the short run.

DEMOCRACY: CONCEPTION AND MISCONCEPTION

Before investigating the nature of democratic change and prospects for democratization in the Arab world, it is necessary to define *democracy*, a notion so appealing to people worldwide that no modern political regime or party has ever declared itself undemocratic or antidemocratic. Either the term itself or the root meaning of democracy, "rule by the people," appears in almost all Arab constitutions. For example, the first articles in the constitutions of Algeria, Egypt, Iraq, and Syria describe the state as a "Democratic and People's Republic," a "democratic, socialist State," a "sovereign, people's, democratic republic," and a "democratic, popular, socialist and sovereign state," respectively.[3] The recent National Charter of Jordan declares the state "a State of Law in the modern sense of a democratic state."[4]

Its tremendous propaganda value notwithstanding, the term "democracy" has meant different things at different periods of history. To Herodotus, it meant "majority rule, equality, and responsibility."[5] Aristotle defined democracy as "a constitution in which the freeborn and poor control the government—being at the same time a majority."[6] The ancient Athenians practiced direct democracy, with all free-born male citizens having an equal voice in the governmental decision-making process. This early form of democracy disappeared, and the term was subsequently applied to modern democracy, the origins of which may be traced to the seventeenth century. Of the modern definitions of democracy, that of contemporary scholar Robert Dahl is one of the most influential.

Dahl considers democracy an ideal political order, which actual democratic systems may never reach.[7] In his most recent "theory of the democratic process," Dahl proposed five criteria for a democratic process: (1) citizens must have adequate and equal opportunities for effective participation, (2) citizens must have voting equality at the decisive stage of collective decisions, (3) citizens must have an enlightened understanding of the matters to be decided, (4) citizens must control the agenda of the matters to be decided, and (5) every sane, adult citizen must be included in the demos.[8]

Recognizing the ideal nature of this notion of democracy, Dahl subsequently developed a concept incorporating the features of existing "democratic" nations. This concept, *polyarchy*, refers to a political system that is characterized by inclusiveness (or high political participation) and public contestation (or the right of citizens to oppose government officials). Polyarchy is an institutional arrangement that attempts to approximate the ideal of democracy. It is characterized by seven institutions that are typical of modern, Western democratic regimes. There is some consensus among scholars that the following institutions, as formulated by Dahl, comprise the minimum requirements for political democracy:

1. Elected officials have a constitutional right to control government policy decisions.
2. Free and fair elections are held regularly under limited government coercion.
3. Universal suffrage is upheld for virtually all adult citizens.
4. All adult, sane, law-abiding citizens have the right to run for public office.
5. Citizens have the right to freedom of expression without risk to their personal freedom or security.
6. Citizens have legal access to nongovernmental sources of information, including sources that oppose the government.
7. Citizens have the right to form independent political parties, associations, and interest groups that can compete in elections.[9]

By contrast, a typical autocracy is headed by a member of the political elite who exercises virtually unlimited, personal power.[10] It is characterized by the considerable restriction of (1) political freedom for all citizens and (2) political participation in which various parties compete freely for influence among the populace, and (3) by the absence of institutional constraints on the power of the chief executive.[11] In the contemporary world, most polities lie somewhere on a continuum between absolute autocracy and democracy; most political systems, including those of the Arab states, contain a variable mix of autocratic and democratic features.[12]

THE ARAB WORLD: FROM TRADITIONAL TO MODERN AUTHORITARIANISM

Regardless of the measures used, none of the Arab states is a polyarchy or meets all of the minimum criteria of democracy as set out by Dahl.[13] A few states meet almost all of the criteria of autocracy, and even the states considered the most democratic fully meet only one of the criteria of democracy, that of "inclusive suffrage." All other criteria are either unsatisfied or only partially satisfied. Incongruity often exists between formal statements and actual practice. Certain aspects of Western democracy are included in most Arab constitutions (equality of citizens before the law, freedom of expression, and freedom of the press); however, their implementation has often been absent, partial, or short-lived.

Nevertheless, most Arab states are adopting some democratic measures. Those that are loosening up their arbitrary, autocratic procedures refer to the process as "democratic" or "democratizing," and scholars studying this phenomenon describe it as "democratization."[14] The concept of democratization, however, refers to a process of transition ending in Western-style democracy, which, in this author's opinion, is a very unlikely outcome. Far more probable is the emergence of a gentler, less traditional type of authoritarianism in which the form or appearance, rather than the substance, of democracy is maintained.

Drawing on the traditional Muslim concept of consultation (*shura*),[15] many modern Arab rulers have created consultative bodies, in some cases through direct elections. Some leaders issued new constitutions, enacted democratic measures, and held elections only to ensure their own political survival, undercut their rivals, and keep their subordinates in line. In general, however, most leaders, instituted these changes in response to demands for political and/or economic reform, which came in the form of public petitions, public meetings, demonstrations, and riots. These leaders have carefully engineered and monitored the implementation of democratic measures: Any attempt by individuals or groups to change the rulers or the political system will be met with firmness and possibly brutality. No Arab regime is ready to yield power to the people in a real democratic transition. The changes have created merely a facade of democracy, superimposed on traditional, authoritarian societies. The majority of people under these "reformed" regimes have little knowledge of Western democracy and are generally ambivalent about Western values, which they sometimes perceive as a threat to their cultural identity.

In the wake of the Gulf War, leaders of Arab regimes were alarmed by renewed domestic demands for liberalization, which were reinforced by Western media calls for democratization, particularly with regard to the Gulf states. Claiming the exigencies of national security, states were able to resist these pressures in the immediate aftermath of the war; subsequently, however, some states have attempted to appease the masses without yielding any significant power. Advisory councils were created or expanded in Oman and the United Arab Emirates, and elections for the National Assembly in Kuwait were held in October 1992. Saudi Arabia promulgated its first written statutes of government in 1992. Yemen and Jordan experienced a continued reduction of arbitrary rule in 1991 and 1992. In April 1993 the newly united Republic of Yemen was planning to hold national elections in which a number of political parties would be competing for popular votes.

By contrast, other states after the war returned to older, nondemocratic forms of rule. After their authority and legitimacy were seriously challenged by Islamic opposition forces, the governments of Tunisia and Algeria cracked down on the fundamentalists, banning their parties and arresting thousands. Egypt's government followed suit after a series of armed assaults by Islamic militants targeted state officials and police, Copts (Egyptian Christians), and anti-fundamentalist activists. Most indicative of the dynamics of political transformation in the Arab world is the Algerian experience, in which the army prevented the Islamists from dominating the legislature by canceling the second round of national elections.

In the following pages, the status of democracy as of January 1993 in Algeria, Egypt, Jordan, Iraq, Kuwait, and Saudi Arabia is examined and assessed in light of Dahl's requirements. In each case, relevant political developments since the country's independence are briefly reviewed.

Algeria

While constitutionally a presidential republic, Algeria is in fact ruled by a military oligarchy that came to power soon after the country's independence from France in 1962. During the protracted and bloody war of liberation, the military provided armed support for the National Liberation Front (FLN). After a brief rule by Ahmad Ben Bella, a civilian leader of the FLN, the military gained political control under the leadership of Hawari Boumedienne, who was later succeeded by Shazli Benjedid. The FLN became a convenient political instrument for this military dictatorship and was used to promote an economic transformation along centralized, socialist lines. The party and the state bureaucracy were dominated by officers who showed little competence for government and who drained the country's rich natural resources, resulting in a large foreign debt, high levels of unemployment, and near bankruptcy.[16] As a consequence, by the late 1980s, the party's popularity had plummeted to such a level that the president found it necessary to

initiate some democratic reforms in order to promote political stability and defuse popular dissent. In 1988, he established a multiparty system. Municipal elections were held in 1990, and the first
parliamentary elections took place in November 1991.

The major opposition party—the Islamic Salvation Front (FIS)—
fared well in the local elections and even better in the first round
of parliamentary elections, in which it won 188 of the 231 seats.
Stunningly, all other parties, including the ruling FLN, were left with
fewer than 50 seats, a clear indication that the elections were not
rigged by the government. Alarmed by the prospect of losing power
to Islamic fundamentalists in the second ballot, the army, which is
the principal beneficiary and the guarantor of the status quo,
launched a preemptive strike on January 12, 1992. It forced the
president to resign, took control of security in the streets, and created a new, five-member governing body—the High Committee of
State (HCS). The HCS, which is still in power, was initially headed by
Muhammad Boudiaf, a former leader of the Algerian revolution drawn
by the generals from a 28-year self-imposed exile in Morocco.[17]
Real power, however, remains in the hands of the military, which is
represented in the HCS by Defense Minister Khalid Nezzar.

Although the democratization process initiated by Benjedid was
endangered by the rise of the FIS, whose leaders include such
staunch opponents of modern democracy as the popular preacher
Ali Belhaj, the usurpation of power by the HCS halted a process
unique to the Arab world, returning Algeria to nondemocratic rule.
The government declared a state of emergency and cracked down
on the FIS, arresting its leaders and cadres[18] and banning religion-
based parties and political activity in mosques and public institutions, notably schools and colleges. Security forces clashed with
Islamic fundamentalists in several cities, resulting in a number of
casualties.[19] The government has been charged with torturing
detainees in the overcrowded desert prison camps.[20] Shortly before
his assassination in June 1992, Boudiaf conceded that 4,214 Algerians remained in those detention camps.[21] The number of detainees
has increased since Ali Kafi assumed chairmanship of the HCS, and
the regime's war against the Islamists continues to rage.

Egypt

Egypt has a multiparty system, yet it remains largely controlled by
a president drawn from the military oligarchy and by his party,
the National Democratic Party (NDP), which dominates both the

People's Assembly and the Shura Council. Three of the other principal political parties are headed by friends of the regime: the Liberal Socialist Party, headed by a former Free Officer supporting free enterprise; the Nationalist Progressive Unionist Rally Party (Tajammu'), headed by a leftist former Free Officer; and the Socialist Labor Party, headed by a former member of a Sadat cabinet.[22] The NDP is favored by electoral law, which requires any party seeking representation in the People's Assembly to obtain at least 8 percent of the total national vote. Votes received by parties that do not reach this threshold are automatically added to the total received by the majority party, which has always been the NDP, so its representation in the assembly is inflated.[23] Elected officials have never differed with the president on issues of national importance, thereby failing to fulfill their role of serving as a check on the personal authority of the chief executive. The president, always nominated by his ruling party in the People's Assembly as the sole presidential candidate, can stay in power indefinitely, ensuring that the fundamental nature of the Egyptian leadership—a popularly supported president with a military background exercising strong personal authority backed by the army—has remained unchanged since 1952.

Egyptian presidents since Gamal Abdel Nasser have made verbal commitments to democratic principles, but these have not been fulfilled. Anwar Sadat's rapprochement with Muslim fundamentalists and other traditional parties of the monarchic era was an attempt to weaken Nasser's political followers, not a reflection of genuine democratic feelings. This fact was clearly demonstrated when Sadat declined to grant the Muslim Brotherhood party legal status and later when he cracked down on dissidents of various faiths and professions, arresting hundreds. Upon assuming office, Hosni Mubarak legalized some of the parties that posed no threat to the regime, excluding the more popular Muslim Brotherhood and, until recently, the Nasserites. He released political prisoners and provided greater freedom of expression in an effort to portray himself as more conciliatory than Sadat. Nevertheless, he wields no less personal authority than did his predecessors. In fact, unlike Nasser and Sadat, Mubarak has not yet appointed a vice president, thereby frustrating the ambitions of other potential leaders.

Since 1981, President Mubarak has maintained a state of emergency, which allows the police to detain people without charge or trial. The Egyptian Organization for Human Rights, which has documented the routine practice of torture by the police over the past 10 years, has concluded that torture is "an officially sanctioned policy in Egypt, particularly towards certain political opposition groups."[24] On December 12, 1991, it launched a one-year campaign of national awareness, the results of which appear to have been negligible.

There is evidence of recurrent electoral fraud, a practice that led large numbers of Egyptians to stay away from the 1990 elections, which were, however, apparently fair.[25] With a low voter turnout (15 percent of the eligible population), and with the major opposition parties boycotting the elections, the government did not encounter, as Salaheddin Hafez of the Egyptian daily *al-Ahram* put it, "enough opposition to make vote-rigging worth the bother."[26]

Radio and television stations, which are owned and run by the state, support government candidates during elections; however, the Egyptian press is relatively free, and licensed opposition papers are allowed to print their viewpoints. The judiciary is also relatively independent of the executive body.[27]

Iraq

Iraq has been ruled by the Ba'ath party since 1968. The executive body is led by the Revolutionary Command Council (RCC), which elects a chairman who becomes president of the republic (Article 37 of the constitution). The president is also the chief of the army and the head of the cabinet, which appoints and dismisses the prime minister, other ministers, and judges. All RCC members "enjoy full immunity. No measures can be taken against any of them without a priori permission of the Council" (Article 40). The RCC has the right to issue laws and decrees (Article 42), declare war, and conclude peace (Article 43).[28]

Legislative power is vested partly in the National Council, which is composed of 250 members elected by universal adult suffrage for a term of four years. The first council was formed in 1980, followed by elections for a 50-member Kurdish legislative council. The third and latest council was elected in 1989. In principle, the major role of the National Council is to consider the draft laws proposed by the RCC or the president, but in fact it has been a rubber stamp for the decrees of the president and the RCC. A new draft constitution, providing for a multiparty system and a half-appointed Consultative Assembly, was approved by the National Assembly in July 1990. Together with the National Assembly, this new body would assume the role of the RCC, which is supposed to be dissolved.[29]

Iraq allows no real opposition groups. Independent candidates for the National Assembly and members of the National Progressive

Front are supporters of the regime, who are carefully screened before being allowed to run for office. Freedom of expression, assembly, and the press do not exist. The state's record of human rights violations is among the world's worst. Amnesty International and other human rights groups report that thousands of political prisoners have been arbitrarily arrested and detained without trial and that torture is widespread, as is the "disappearance" of people, many feared dead. Hundreds have been reported executed, often without judicial order.

Jordan

Jordan has taken important steps away from the absolute monarchic rule that has prevailed since the country's independence in 1946. The first direct elections since 1967 were held in 1989. Although political parties were still banned, about 63 percent of eligible voters elected 22 members of the Muslim Brotherhood, which concealed its status as a political party while operating as a charity, and 12 independents who sympathize with the party. Together they comprise a third of the lower house. The role of the House of Deputies in the formulation of government policy decisions has been enhanced. By slowly implementing more democratic measures, the regime appears to have gained more self-confidence, stability, and popularity, despite the economic problems brought about by the Gulf War and by its tense relationship with the Arab Gulf states and Egypt.[30]

Martial law was suspended in 1990 and subsequently abolished in April 1992. Security restrictions on travel and employment for political activists were canceled. Some political parties were legalized. Freedom of expression and assembly have expanded and press censorship has been much reduced.[31] In 1991, King Hussein bin Talal approved the National Charter, drafted by a 60-member commission. The charter provides for political pluralism, respect for human rights, and support for self-government in the provinces. It considers "the democratic revolution" one of the challenges of the twenty-first century.[32]

Nevertheless, the country remains a hereditary monarchy. The Jordanian constitution stipulates that the throne of the kingdom must be held by a male descendent of the late King Abdullah Ibn al-Hussein, and provides specific rules of succession. The king has both legislative and executive authorities. He shares the former with the National Assembly, which is composed of the elected House of Deputies and an appointed Senate, while the latter is exercised through a cabinet of ministers. The king may dissolve the National Assembly and appoint and dismiss the prime minister and any or all the ministers.[33]

Although Jordan's constitutional monarchy incorporates more democratic measures than most other Arab countries, it is far from polyarchy; the extent of opposition that can be tolerated by the government is clearly limited. This was demonstrated when the parliamentary opposition, dominated by the Muslim Brotherhood, forced Taher al-Masri's cabinet to resign but did not dare challenge the king's cousin when he was nominated premier, despite their opposition to his opinions regarding the Middle East peace process and the application of Islam to Jordanian society. In the summer of 1992, two Islamist members of parliament (MPs), Laith Shbeilat and Ya'qub Qarsh, were arrested and convicted of conspiracy against the state. After many requests from local and international Islamic groups, the king intervened to suspend the sentences and release Shbeilat and Qarsh.[34]

Kuwait

Like Jordan, Kuwait is a hereditary monarchy. Its constitution stipulates that the ruler must be a descendent of the late Prince Mubarak al-Sabah, who died in 1915. The Kuwaiti constitution also provides for an elected National Assembly, although this provision was suspended in 1985, followed by other restrictions on political freedom. At the end of the Iran–Iraq war in 1988, public demand for the restoration of the assembly intensified, with about 40 percent of the electorate petitioning for its recall. The emir promised only that discussions would be held, while the police forcibly stopped rallies (*diwaniyyas*) at the homes of former deputies. A new prodemocracy movement, the Constitutional Movement, was formed, composed of outspoken citizens and a number of assembly members, who demanded the reinstatement of the National Assembly. In June 1990, elections were held for a National Council, consisting of 50 elected and 25 appointed members. A number of political groups, including 27 members of the suspended assembly, boycotted the elections, claiming that the new council violated the constitution and "distracted attention from real democratic demands."[35]

During the Iraqi occupation of Kuwait, the crown prince made a pledge to about 700 Kuwaitis in Jeddah, Saudi Arabia, to "solidify democracy and deepen popular participation" once Kuwait was freed.[36] After the liberation, the emir promised to hold elections promptly, but they were repeatedly postponed until October 1992, when 50 out of 279 candidates to the National Assembly were freely and fairly elected. The opposition parties won 72 percent of the seats (36 seats), half of which went to the Islamists (both Sunni and Shiite), and the other half to the liberals and reformists. Two of the Democratic Platform leaders, Ahmad al-Khatib and Abdullah al-Nibari, were elected, along with 10 members of the Constitutional Movement, including its leader Ahmad al-Sa'adoon.[37]

Despite some recent relaxation, the restrictions on freedom of expression and assembly, as well as press censorship, remain significant. The police and government-sponsored armed civilians have perpetrated all sorts of atrocities against expatriates accused of collaboration with the Iraqi forces during the occupation. Human rights groups in Kuwait have reported flagrant violations of basic human rights, particularly towards Palestinians. Evidence shows that routine torture in Kuwait has resulted in scores of deaths.

At present, Kuwait does not qualify as a democracy on the basis of any of Dahl's criteria. Even the criterion of inclusive suffrage, which is applicable to several other Arab countries, is not met. Under the present electoral law, the right of suffrage is limited to the small segment of male citizens over the age of 21 whose ancestors lived in Kuwait prior to 1920. As a result, Kuwait is an oligarchy in which only 9 percent (81,938)[38] of all citizens have the right to vote.

Saudi Arabia

After 60 years of al-Saud rule, King Fahd bin Abdulaziz issued three statutes that comprise the first written set of rules of government in the history of Saudi Arabia. The first extends the eligibility for succession to the Saudi throne to the younger sons and grandsons of the late King Abdulaziz al-Saud, thereby appeasing the young princes. It also guarantees individual rights of freedom, private property, and privacy. The second establishes a Consultative or Shura Council with limited advisory powers. The council members are to be selected by the king. The kingdom also has an elaborate tribal system of consultation, under which the royal princes and the king hold weekly (and sometimes more frequent) audiences in order to receive citizen grievances and requests. Each prince has a number of assistants who help him resolve these issues. The third statute grants additional power to the provinces directly governed by royal princes.

Although the political changes embodied in the three new statutes of government fall far below Western, and perhaps even Saudi liberal expectations, they are significant in that they represent an unprecedented effort to legitimize the coexistence of a civil, manmade constitution with the godly law of *shari'a* in Islamic communities, a possibility that was previously rejected by the Saudi leadership. Despite official statements that the statutes do not constitute a constitution,[39] most of their articles bear a strong resemblance to those of other Arab states, which label their statutes "constitution." King Fahd clearly understood the significance of the step that he was taking, as he felt compelled to dispel the fears of pious Wahhabis about the direction of social and political change in Saudi Arabia by stating:

> The democratic system prevalent in the world is not appropriate for us in this region. . . . The election system has no place in the Islamic creed, which calls for a government of advice and consultation and for the shepherd's openness to his flock, and holds the ruler fully responsible before his people.[40]

Although these changes were promised by the king 10 years ago, the unprecedented level of popular demands in the wake of the war no doubt accelerated their enactment. Coming about one year after the end of the Gulf War, they represent a positive step in the political history of Saudi Arabia, opening a window of opportunity for further changes toward a kinder, less traditional form of authoritarianism. They acknowledge the legitimacy both of the demands of the younger al-Saud princes, who want a larger share of the power now concentrated in the hands of the sons of Abdulaziz, an aging, degenerating oligarchy, and of the demands of professionals, intellectuals, and clerics who are seeking political reform.[41] They recognize the necessity of departing from oral traditions of tribal politics with regard to the rules of succession to the throne. The enactment of specified, written rules brings Saudi Arabia into line with the non-Gulf Arab monarchies of Jordan and Morocco. While maintaining the authoritarian leadership of the royal princes in the provinces, they allow citizens a greater voice in the management of local affairs. They limit the arbitrary rule of the religious police, commonly known as *mutawwi'in*, by making clear provisions regarding private property, privacy, and personal freedom. Both foreigners and Saudis have repeatedly complained of police excesses in the enforcement of Islamic codes of conduct, including the beating, whipping, and sometimes the detention of violators. Although women will remain veiled and segregated from men, they will at least be able to enjoy some measure of privacy in their homes without fear of unannounced raids by the *mutawwi'in*. As the new statutes are implemented, harassment of women and foreigners in public places is also likely to decrease.

Nevertheless, immense power remains in the hands of the monarch. The political system does not provide for elections, political parties, labor unions, strikes or demonstrations, freedom of expression, or public observance of religion other than Islam. The judiciary, which is Islamic, is independent, but trials are closed.[42] All printed matter is censored. Radio and television are tightly controlled public agencies. Non-Saudi, as well as Saudi, women have very restricted freedom and are the principal target of harassment by the religious police. They are not permitted to work alongside men, they cannot drive, and they are not allowed to travel without a male relative. Saudi women are prohibited from marrying non-Saudis without the prior consent of their government, a restriction that does not apply to Saudi men.

PROSPECTS FOR DEMOCRACY IN THE ARAB WORLD

The institution of democratic principles in the Arab world has reduced the arbitrariness of authoritarian regimes, thereby making countries such as Egypt, Jordan, Kuwait, and Yemen neither totally autocratic nor close to being polyarchic. The emerging political systems are a hybrid of democracy and autocracy or theocracy. Such forms may not be as unstable and transitory as the noted social scientist Philippe Schmitter asserts.[43] If major world religions can survive centuries of political and social transformation by making some adaptive changes, it seems that traditional polities should be able to withstand storms of political upheaval that call for democratization by introducing certain limited liberal or democratic measures.

Certainly, there are a host of factors that militate against the peaceful transition to full-fledged democracy in the region. Notable among these—and, indeed, often cited among the conditions that may enhance or hamper the transition to democracy[44]—are the nature of the state and political leadership, the characteristics of the prevailing social structure and political culture, and the role of external forces.

State and Leadership

In the years since the 1973 Arab-Israeli war, the great majority of Arab political regimes have shown remarkable resilience despite numerous diplomatic failures, major military defeats, and, for the non-oil-exporting countries, serious economic problems. The eminent Middle Eastern historian Albert Hourani adapted the ideas of Ibn Khaldun, the great medieval Arab scholar, to explain this stability in terms of three factors: the cohesiveness of the ruling group, its alliance with powerful social classes or interest groups, and the presence of powerful ideas or ideologies that legitimize the rulers.[45] The cohesion of the ruling groups is due, in part, to the unprecedented strength of their instruments of repression. Several disciplined and loyal agencies and forces—army, police, civil security agency (*mukhabarat*), military security forces, foreign mercenaries—have been systematically used to control the masses. Opposition is silenced either by bribery, where possible, or by ruthless suppression: jailing, torture, or assassination. Rulers have also maintained power by means of alliances with tribal, communal, ethnic, or sectarian groups, and/or with political factions and power bases in the armed forces. Although the primary source of the strength of the state varies from one country to another, "ties of interest" within states are always bolstered by those of "neighborliness, kinship or intermarriage."[46]

Algeria has been ruled by a military oligarchy in collaboration with the ruling party, the FLN. This regime found strong allies among emerging business entrepreneurs and public officials of the rapidly growing civil bureaucracy created to support the development of a highly centralized, socialist economy. When Benjedid's multiparty system failed to support the political status quo, the army, to protect its vested interests and interests of other influential social groups in the bureaucracy and the society at large, replaced him, thereby reasserting its constitutionally granted role as the protector of the status quo.

In Egypt, the ruling military oligarchy firmly controls both the armed forces and security agencies. Its lower-middle-class origins allow the oligarchy to appeal to the values and sentiments of the poor and middle classes and establish a strong alliance with the middle class.[47] Under Nasser, this alliance was based primarily on ties with the rural middle class, as most of the Free Officers were of rural origin. As the state bureaucracy expanded, it was broadened to include much of the urban middle class, which was rapidly absorbed into the state agencies. Egyptian state ideology appealed not only to the values of the poor and middle classes, but also, lately, to the values of the nouveaux riches. Under Nasser, ideology was based on the ideals of freedom, socialism, and Arab unity. Sadat promised people prosperity under *infitah* (opening), while Mubarak pledged to prosecute the "fat cats" generated by Sadat's "opening" and establish "democracy, development, security, and purity," as opposed to corruption.[48]

Iraqi society and politics are characterized by a pervasive clannishness, extending from the ruling Takritis downward.[49] The Iraqi leadership is a close kinship group of peasant origin, which firmly controls the ruling Ba'ath party, the armed forces, and the security agencies. This group has established a strong alliance with the Sunni population, particularly the rural middle class, and a significant sector of the Shi'is, who constitute the rank-and-file of the state bureaucracy. Saddam Hussein has managed to hold the armed forces together, despite the terrible toll of his wars, by instituting various means of control, including indoctrination with Ba'ath ideology and the establishment of intelligence bodies linked to him.[50] The state ideology of pan-Arabism appeals to the sentiments of wide sectors of the population, and one of the founders of the Ba'ath, Michele Aflaq, remained a highly venerated figure until his death.

The royal Hashemite family of Jordan is strongly cohesive, with established practices of rule that are in part legitimated by descent from the Prophet Muhammad. It also derives a large measure of strength from ties to the Bedouins, who dominate the armed forces and who have repeatedly demonstrated deep loyalty to the king.[51] At the same time, the ruling family is able to draw on a wider and far less conservative social base; Palestinians, who now constitute the overwhelming majority of the population, have shown continuous support. Even in the late 1970s, when the PLO was at the height of its power, most Palestinians remained either supportive of, or neutral towards, the regime because of vested economic and political interests.

The Kuwaiti royal family is a cohesive ruling group within the small indigenous population (under 800,000). Its power stems from alliances with families of leading merchants in the emirate. The extensive welfare state established by the Sabahs is another important source of strength. Kuwait's oil wealth has allowed its rulers to provide citizens with a wide range of social benefits. It also enabled the ruling family to use "rentier politics," that is to bribe local and regional opponents with large amounts of money in order to win their goodwill.[52] Before the Gulf War, the Sabahs portrayed themselves as pan-Arab and pan-Islamic, dispensing generous aid to other Arab and Islamic states. Today, the security and sovereignty of the state are paramount, thus the leadership has moderated its pan-Islamic and pan-Arab stances.

Saudi Arabia is a monarchy headed by a large tribe with a few thousand princes. The polity is based on long-established and extremely elaborate patron-client networks between members of the royal family and ordinary citizens, which permit the citizenry to share in the country's wealth, albeit quite inequitably. Strong alliances also exist between the rulers and influential social groups, notably, the clerics (*ulema*), businessmen, intellectuals, and chiefs of other tribes. The ideological base of the kingdom is a mixture of tribal values and those of the puritan Wahhabi sect of Islam.

The process of social transformation in Arab countries has radically altered the role of the state, which is now a much more pervasive force than it was two decades ago in the everyday life of the average citizen.[53] Government expenditures often exceed 50 percent of GDP,[54] and bureaucracies have grown so immense that in some countries two or more employees are assigned the task of one, a situation that inevitably leads to inefficiency and job dissatisfaction. In some cases, the total number of active and retired civilian and military government employees, together with their dependents, exceeds one quarter of the population.[55]

Arab governments remain the principal economic actors, maintaining traditional patron-client relationships with their members and supporters. They grant contracts to valued clients who, in turn, pay government officials handsome commissions. With few exceptions, these "kickbacks" have been implicitly integrated into the code of business transactions between governments and private enterprises, both domestic and foreign. Economic privatization measures have been enacted in the past decade by some Arab states to favor those sectors of society that have vested interests in the maintenance of the prevailing regimes; major beneficiaries have been present and former state officials, army generals, and capitalists who have demonstrated continuous loyalty to the political leadership.

Arab political leadership remains personal, authoritarian, patrimonial, and patriarchal, despite the considerable social and economic change that the region has undergone. Whether the leader comes from a minority or a majority group, from one sect or another, whether he is of rural or urban origin, a king or a president, and whether or not he describes himself as "democratic" makes little difference. The basic set of leadership qualities are amazingly similar across the Arab Middle East. So much personal power is vested in each Arab political leader that he becomes the most important symbol of his nation, with many people apprehensive of the future in the event of his death. Death is the usual means by which authority is transferred; it is allowed to come naturally in monarchies and is all too frequently inflicted by a rival in coups d'état of republics. Patterns of leadership in secular parties are closely related to the nature of the social structure and to the prevalent political culture.

Social Structure

Arab societies incorporate strong kinship, communal, and sectarian bonds. Kinship takes the traditional form of tribalism (*qabiliyya*) or the less traditional form of extended familism (*'ailiyya*). The influence of the family on the life of the individual supersedes that of all other social institutions, including the state. Special relations and strong loyalty exist between people who come from the same village, town, or city quarter. Strong allegiance to the members of one's religious sect is displayed regardless of whether or not one actively engages in the practice of religious rites. It is these kinship, communal, and sectarian affiliations, and not individual personality, that constitute the basis of a citizen's identity. This social structure, which Hisham Sharabi calls "neopatriarchy," also incorporates an ethos of subordination and hierarchy, which hinders the development of nationalist consciousness.[56]

It is clear that Arab societies lack the features of a civil society that prevail in all stable democracies and that have, in many cases, preceded the transition to democracy. It is hardly surprising that Arab societies lack a civil society, which is a rather recent Western invention. "Civil society" refers to the presence of intermediary units that mediate between the state agencies and the primary social units such as individuals, families, and sects. According to Schmitter, the intermediary units in a fully developed civil society such as voluntary associations, labor unions, and syndicates are characterized by (1) independence from state institutions as well as primary units, (2) self-organization and a corporate status that is recognized and protected by the state, and (3) the capacity to govern their members.[57] Without such autonomous groups, societies are more likely to be dominated by a nondemocratic, centralized state.[58]

Apparently cognizant that the development of a civil society would pose a threat to their authoritarianism, Arab regimes have sought either to destroy[59] or to coopt autonomous social groups. When such groups proved amenable to control by the state apparatus, including the ruling party and security agencies, they continued to operate, albeit only as part of the huge state bureaucracy.

Throughout the Arab world, single-party regimes have seized control of various "popular" organizations such as the peasants', laborers', teachers', physicians', and women's unions and associations and turned them into mouthpieces for the regimes and useful instruments to contain and suppress popular dissent. However, when autonomous organizations insisted on maintaining their independence from the state, they were eventually forcibly disbanded or outlawed. The banning through legal procedures in July 1991 of the Tunisian human rights organization, one of the oldest in the region, is a case in point.

The existence of an independent bourgeoisie is sometimes considered essential to the development of a civil society. Despite economic modernization efforts, such a social class is yet to emerge in the Arab countries, where entrepreneurs and businessmen remain heavily dependent either on their state or on the bourgeoisie of Western states. This, together with other factors analyzed herein, may explain the failure of Arab states to develop democracy.

Political Culture

The compatibility of Islam and Western democracy has been the subject of heated debates for decades, with no resolution in sight. Many Western thinkers believe that the Muslim Arab culture, which dominates Arab societies, is antidemocratic or "not hospitable to democracy."[60] Samuel Huntington has noted that democracy is highly correlated with Protestantism and well tolerated by the oriental cultures of Hindu and Shinto. However, he considers Islam to be hostile to democracy, in part because it does not distinguish between religion and politics. Islam has also been portrayed as intolerant of alien ideas and diversity of beliefs and values.

One problem with such generalizations is the confusion between Islam as a universal religion and civilization and the nondemocratic practices of Muslim political leaders in so-called Islamic states. Certainly, Muslim despots, many Muslim clerics (*'ulema*), and some Islamic radical movements accept the widespread Western contention that Islam and democracy are antithetical, but many others have different points of view.

Islamic law (*shari'a*) is comprised of two basic sources: the Koran (a revealed text) and the Sunna (the sayings—*hadiths*—and exemplary behavior of the Prophet Muhammad). The Koran and the Sunna advocate the practice of consultation (*shura*) among Muslims and order the Prophet to consult with his companions,[61] thus providing the Islamic concept closest to that of modern democracy. Given the nature of shura and the diversity of views concerning other philosophical and political matters that are closely related to the concept of democracy, Islamists are bound to differ about the compatibility of Islam and Western democracy. These differences are reflected in *fatawa* (judgmental opinions), which allow a wide range of political systems to invoke Islam in legitimation of their authority.

Opinion is divided among three broad categories. The first, which views Islam and democracy as either totally or largely incompatible, is referred to here as "fundamentalist." Although the term fundamentalism is alien to Islamic civilization and can be misleading, it is nevertheless used here for want of a better alternative. It implies a rigid, constrictive interpretation and strict adherence to the letter of the *shari'a*. The second position finds Islam and democracy highly compatible, and will thus be called "liberal." The third is an eclectic, intermediate position. It includes diverse interpretations of Islam in which only a few democratic ideals and institutions are accepted.

By its very nature, a fundamentalist interpretation of religion renders its proponents, be they Muslims, Christians, or Jews, largely intolerant of different beliefs and outlooks, a point of view that is incompatible with democracy. By contrast, proponents of Islamic liberalism believe that the *shari'a* introduced general principles of governance: consultation, justice, freedom of faith, and equality among nations and races,[62] leaving Islamic civilization and religion free to embrace any political system. This liberal school was influenced by decades of interaction between the Arab world and Western culture, which led to the Westernization of many members of the elite in Arab countries.

The majority of Islamic groups, jurists, and thinkers are ambivalent toward Western democracy, neither rejecting it entirely nor fully endorsing it. Although they all believe in the unity of religion and state in Islam, and that the *shari'a* should be a main source of legislation in Muslim societies, they adopt those democratic principles they view as consistent with Islamic tenets. This heterogeneous group holds a wide array of viewpoints regarding democracy, ranging from that of the mainstream Muslim Brotherhood to that of traditional, religious Muslim laymen who practice rituals with little understanding of the broader issues of religion, philosophy, and politics. A large segment of sheikhs, *'ulema,* and imams (notably in the Azhar of Egypt, the distinguished academy of higher learning in Sunni Islam) are also tolerant of democracy.

In short, although the fundamentalist position is gaining ground among the Muslim masses of several countries as an avenue for dissent (see chapter 4), the belief that Islam and Western democracy are antithetical is by no means common to all Muslim thinkers. Advocates for each of the multitude of view points invoke *fatawa* in support of their positions, and political culture is dominated by a moderate, middle-ground attitude toward democracy.[63] However, due to its basic conservatism and resistance to innovative ideas and practices, this political culture is not yet hospitable to a polyarchic order. Democracy is, after all, a very radical departure from centuries-old Arab political traditions of authoritarianism and political apathy. Although not characteristic of Islam per se, these qualities do create a very real, though by no means insurmountable, obstacle to democratization in Muslim Arab societies, and it will take them some time to appreciate the benefits of democracy over traditional authoritarianism.

External Forces

External factors can have a significant impact on the process of social transformation. For example, democratic parties and governments in Europe contributed to the emergence of democratic institutions in nondemocratic parts of the continent.[64] Some analysts maintain that one such factor, colonialism, was instrumental in the worldwide expansion of democracy.[65] The linkage of Western economic aid to the implementation of some democratic measures in nondemocratic states also helped reduce the arbitrariness of autocratic rule. Proponents of this point of view are opposed by "dependency" theorists who regard external forces as obstacles to, rather than promoters of, democracy in the Third World.

In Arab countries, the record of external intervention for the purpose of promoting or supporting prodemocracy groups is far from consistent. During the last two decades, the most powerful polyarchy in the world, the United States, either did not try or else failed to foster polyarchy in any Arab country. Dahl put the matter plainly: "The policies of the dominant country are likely to be influenced more strongly by strategic, economic, and geographic considerations than by any special preference for democracy."[66] Thus, when the United States intervened militarily in Kuwait and economically and politically in other Arab countries, it served to strengthen oligarchies and dictatorships at the expense of prodemocracy groups and a potentially autonomous national bourgeoisie.

CONCLUSION

Given the overwhelming power of the centralized Arab state over various aspects of people's lives, the authoritarian nature of political leadership, the strength of kinship and sectarian ties, the absence of a civil society, the ambivalence of the majority of Muslim Arabs toward Western democracy, and the lack of continuous, strong external support for democracy, there seems little chance for Western democracy to develop and prosper in the Arab world, at least in the short run. It is true that in four countries—Jordan, Yemen, and, to a lesser extent, Egypt and Kuwait—there are signs of movement in the direction of democratization, but even there the movement is slow and unsure. Arab polyarchy appears unlikely to evolve until human rights are respected, state forces of repression are neutralized or dispersed, and prodemocratic interpretations of Islam (what Leonard Binder calls "Islamic liberalism")[67] enjoy widespread support.

four

The Decline of Pan-Arabism
and the Rise of Islamism

꧁꧂ Of the various ideological currents that have swept across
the Arab world since World War II, pan-Arabism and
Islamism have proven the most powerful. Proponents of both ideologies have sought to interpret reality to satisfy the self-image of
their target populations.[1] The changes wrought in that "reality" by
the Gulf War have not altered the direction but rather have accentuated the strength of the ideological tide in the Arab world.

Pan-Arabism, or at least that version propounded by Nasser and
by the Ba'ath party in Iraq and Syria, sought to blend together
socialism, Arab nationalism, and secularism. For several decades
this formulation enjoyed substantial popular and political support,
but its consistent failure to translate its idealistic vision into practice
eventually undermined its appeal. The severe blow dealt to Arab unity
by Egypt's signing a peace treaty with Israel in 1978 dealt an equally
severe blow to pan-Arabism, which has been in decline ever since.

In its place has arisen Islamism. Like pan-Arabism, Islamism
sprang in part from hostility to the spread of Western influence and
culture. Unlike pan-Arabism, however, Islamism seeks not a single
unified Arab state but rather the establishment of Islamic theocracies in Muslim countries. Another difference between the two is that
whereas pan-Arabism was embraced by a number of Arab regimes
as well as by substantial sections of their publics, Islamism enjoys
significantly less endorsement from the political elites and has instead become the most potent ideology of popular dissent. In fact,
while Islamism has enjoyed increasing support among the Islamic

masses, many of their elites have turned from pan-Arabism to territorial nationalism.

This chapter examines the conflicting fortunes of these ideologies, looking first at pan-Arabism and then at the surge of Islamism, paying particular attention to the recent political activity of Islamists in Egypt, Jordan, and Algeria. As will be discussed, the impact of the Gulf War has been to underscore, rather than undermine, the strength of Islamism and the redundancy of pan-Arabism.

THE RISE AND DECLINE OF PAN-ARABISM

Pan-Arabism (the term is used interchangeably here with Arabism and Arab nationalism to describe *al-qawmiyya al-'Arabiyya*) is based on the concept of the Arab nation (*al-Umma al-'Arabiyya*), which first appeared late in the nineteenth century. A call for Arab unity was followed by the establishment of secret societies in Lebanon and Syria, which appealed to the Arabs to revolt against Turkish rule. Although these societies soon disbanded, they were succeeded by other groups supporting Arab unity. When World War I began, various Arab nationalist groups joined forces under Sharif Hussein bin Ali of Mecca. In 1915, they issued the Damascus Protocol, in which they demanded an independent Arab state in return for revolting against the Ottomans. The British, represented by Sir Henry McMahon, their high commissioner for Egypt and the Sudan, accepted the terms of the protocol;[2] however, while negotiating with Hussein, the British made secret commitments to the French in the Sykes-Picot Agreement of 1916 and to the Zionist movement in the Balfour Declaration of 1917. Under the terms of the Sykes-Picot Agreement, the British and the French agreed to divide the Arab territories, then under Ottoman rule, between them, creating a number of mandates. The Balfour Declaration pledged British support for the creation of a Jewish homeland in Palestine.

A year later, these two secret commitments became known to Arab nationalist leaders, who were outraged at Britain's total disregard for their aspirations and its nullification of pledges made to Sharif Hussein. They met in Syria in 1919 as the "General Syrian Congress." The Congress rejected the Sykes-Picot Agreement, the Balfour Declaration, and the proposed mandates, and declared instead the independence of Syria and Iraq. The Syria of 1919 included the territories of today's Syria, Lebanon, Jordan, and Israel. In 1920, the Allies met in San Remo and decided to implement the mandate system, thereby determining the political boundaries of most of the present Arab states, and creating deep and long-lasting popular resentment.[3]

The establishment of the mandate system, together with Western recognition of the Zionist movement, contributed to the growth of pan-Arabism in the interwar period.[4] Its growth was also spurred by two factors militating against the development and popular acceptance of strong, sovereign Arab nation-states. In the first place, the notion of internal sovereignty, which requires a sense of citizenship and civic allegiance, and that of external sovereignty,[5] which implies the acceptance of recently established political borders, were new to the region and conflicted with its organization along ethnic, sectarian, and tribal lines.[6] Thus, while the Europeans were able to construct a new territorial map, imposing "Westphalian" nation-states on the Middle East, these states were only nominally sovereign. As the prominent British sociologist Anthony Giddens notes,

> A state can only be sovereign . . . if large segments of the population of that state have mastered an array of concepts connected with sovereignty (such as the notion of citizenship). . . . In many cases the mass of the population of traditional states did not know of themselves to be citizens of those states, nor did it matter particularly to the continuity of power with them.[7]

In the second place, both the traditional and the radical fundamentalist interpretations of Islam find the concept of man's sovereignty incompatible with monotheism. In the words of Abul A'la al-Mawdudi, the leading theoretician of Islamic fundamentalism:

> Nothing can claim sovereignty be it a human being, a family, a class or group of people, or even the human race in the world as a whole. God alone is the Sovereign and His Commandments are the Law of Islam.[8]

Given these considerations, it is not surprising that, as the Arab states acquired independence in the years between 1943 and 1961, they experienced protracted violence and successive coups d'état.[9] Nor is it surprising that it was also during this period that the notion of a single, unified Arab state began to gain the wide popular appeal that allowed it to dominate Middle East politics from the mid-1950s to the late 1960s. During this time, the speeches of President Nasser of Egypt, the foremost pan-Arab leader, were heard all over the Arab world. His calls for freedom from foreign rule, for socialism, and for Arab unity received warm support from substantial segments of the Arab populations. Pan-Arab regimes came to power in Egypt, Syria, Iraq, and Libya. Pan-Arabism also exerted a powerful influence on the Palestinian armed movement.

However, despite its popular appeal, pan-Arabism in all of its forms (Egyptian Nasserism, Syrian and Iraqi Ba'athism) had serious shortcomings. To begin with, it was overly idealistic, offering few feasible economic, political, or organizational programs, and failing to take into account the genuine political, economic, and social differences between Arab countries. In reality, once the new political entities were set up, they strove to establish legitimacy by emphasizing their distinctive local characteristics. National folklore in the forms of dress, dance, and art was revived; and governments undertook archaeological excavations in an effort to establish historical links to pre-Arab and pre-Islamic times. Even postage stamps emphasized territorial themes.[10]

From the outset, Arab political leaders had "a collective interest in maintaining the territorial basis of their political existence,"[11] a fact that is reflected in the pact of the Arab League, which guarantees the sovereignty of member states while "creating the facade of a movement toward unity."[12] Each of the Arab states has developed its own form of centralized bureaucracy and its own national armed forces to safeguard itself from domestic rebellion and external incursion. Even the states' economic systems "often resist integration and manifest protectionist tendencies dictated by particular needs and peculiarities."[13] As a result, the prevailing state systems in the Arab world have been strengthened, and attempts to change the territorial map by uniting two or more Arab countries have generally proved to be futile.[14]

In addition, when confronted with the dilemma of modernizing their societies while retaining traditional religious values, pan-Arab leaders failed to devise a formula reconciling *shari'a* and Western secularism. As a result, many Western-educated Arabs live in two cultural worlds, but are unable to identify completely with either. According to students of the Arab psyche, many Arabs suffer from *izdiwaj*, or split personality, arising from the conflict between the values of Western culture and those of Muslim Arab culture. For example, in his studies of Iraqi society, sociologist Ali al Wardi found many individuals struggling to reconcile the values of their Bedouin heritage, which places great importance on pride and courage, with the submission and endurance required of modern town dwellers.[15] At its extreme, the conflict between traditional and modern values can lead to what Albert Hourani describes as a state of Levantine marginality engendered when an individual can no longer create, but is

> only able to imitate, and not even to imitate correctly, since that also needs a certain originality. It is to belong to no community and to

possess nothing of one's own. It reveals itself in lostness, pretentious-
ness, cynicism and despair.[16]

Because of these shortcomings, in the early 1960s, the pan-Arab
movement began to lose popular support to non-Arabist appeals for
territorial nationalism and state sovereignty. The 1961 failure of the
union between Egypt and Syria was a grave setback, as were the
defeat of the Arab armies in the 1967 Arab-Israeli war and the death
of Nasser in 1971.

Pan-Arabism enjoyed a brief renaissance in 1973–74, a period of
improved coordination among Arab states. President Sadat of Egypt
won wide support for the concerted military assault on Israel in
1973, which was followed by the Arab oil embargo. However, Syria
resented Sadat's unilateral actions during war, and rifts in the Arab
ranks became visible as Sadat proceeded with his peace initiative with
Israel, concluding with the ratification of the Camp David Accords.

The accords marked a turning point for pan-Arabism, the influence of which has since suffered a steady decline. Most Arab governments rejected the accords, regarding them as a separate peace
deal between Egypt and Israel aimed at creating new disputes
among the Arabs. From 1978 until the Gulf crisis, the Arab world
was in disarray. Conflicts erupted between pairs of states, and small
clusters of states formed separate blocs, while Iraq conducted a
devastating eight-year war with Iran, draining its resources and
weakening the economies of the Arab Gulf states that supported it.

Pan-Arabism was further weakened by the collapse of the Soviet
Union and the liberation of Eastern Europe. The Soviet Union and
its Warsaw Pact allies had served as arms suppliers and ideological
models to several parties and states in the Arab world. Their demise
discredited communist and socialist ideologies throughout the Middle East, including the socialism of Nasserite and Ba'athist pan-
Arabism. The refusal of other Arab governments to support Saddam
Hussein's actions against Kuwait and Israel during the 1990–91
Gulf crisis undermined the influence of pan-Arabism still further.
Egypt and the Arab regimes in the Gulf openly declared their unequivocal commitment to national sovereignty and their firm belief
in the permanence of the political borders established by the European powers.

Ultimately, pan-Arabism could not fulfill its early promises. It
raised expectations without satisfying them, resulting in high levels
of popular frustration; and, on more than one occasion, it was
appropriated by governments that not only lacked vision and

experience, but also were more concerned with the expansion of territorial borders than with altruistic cooperation among their fellow Arabs. Hourani contends that pan-Arabism turned into

> slogans which grew stale by repetition, and could no longer gather other ideas around them into a powerful constellation, mobilize social forces for action, or turn power into legitimate authority . . . the main function of Arabism was as a weapon in conflicts between Arab states and a pretext for the interference of one state in the affairs of others.[17]

Nevertheless, the desire for cooperation among Arab peoples still runs deep,[18] particularly in the Fertile Crescent, where Iraq and Syria appear to have maintained a myth[19] of their shared history that tends toward transnationalism. As aptly stated by the scholar Carl Brown:

> The political and intellectual leaders and opinion molders of the Fertile Crescent have been reluctant to accept the legitimacy of the present political arrangement. The prevailing opinion among Fertile Crescent Arabs can be compared to that in Italy or Germany before unification during the last century. There is a generalized desire to do away with existing "artificial" political borders to be replaced by a political entity that is larger, stronger and can command greater loyalty.[20]

THE SURGE OF ISLAMISM

Islamism (also referred to as pan-Islamism or political Islam) has as its goal the establishment of an Islamic state on the basis of the Koran and the Sunna. Like pan-Arabism, Islamism first appeared in response to the introduction of Western influence into the Arab world. However, unlike the pan-Arabists, most pan-Islamic leaders reject the notion of a single unified state, seeking instead to establish Islamic theocracies in countries where Muslims constitute the majority of the population.

The first major Islamic party was the Muslim Brotherhood. Founded in Egypt in 1929 by Hasan al-Banna, it became a tightly organized political movement, striving to establish a theocratic state. The Brethren were not hesitant to engage in acts of violence. Egyptian governments in the late 1940s, and those under Nasser, cracked down on the Brotherhood, greatly weakening its influence. Upon his accession to power, Sadat released members of the Brethren from prisons, allowing them to reorganize and participate in the political process. Although not granted legal status, the Brethren were allowed to run for office under the auspices of any of the legal parties. As a result, support, especially among the young, for the Muslim Brotherhood and other Islamic movements increased not only in Egypt but also in other Arab countries.

The recent history of the Arab world has been marked by a recurrence of military defeats, economic disasters, and bloody internecine conflicts. The gap between the rich and the poor within each country has widened, with ever-increasing numbers of people living at subsistence levels while others have acquired unprecedented wealth.[21] Conflict between Arab states has been the norm and cooperation the exception. Political repression predominates, while national heritage, traditions, and traditional values—particularly those concerning religion and community—are being increasingly displaced by modern, Western practices.

Nevertheless, Islam remains a basic component of both personal and national identity, and Islamic fundamentalism[22] has found widespread support among the unemployed, the alienated, the frustrated, and the repressed. During the 1970s and 1980s, Islam was used as a political weapon in various struggles against perceived sources of social injustice, inequality, atheism, or political suppression, most notably in Iran and in Egypt, where fundamentalist elements considered Sadat to be "the Pharaoh."

The power of Islamic symbolism was once again manifested during the Gulf crisis. Saddam Hussein suddenly shed his secular Arabist garb and called for an Islamic *jihad* (holy war) against the Western, non-Muslim troops that "occupied" the Muslims' holy land. This call, combined with a proposed linkage between his withdrawal from Kuwait and Israel's withdrawal from the occupied Arab territories, struck a resonant chord in the Muslim Arab psyche.

Cognizant of the power of Islamic symbols and the implications of his self-proclaimed role as "custodian of the two holy mosques," King Fahd of Saudi Arabia responded skillfully. First, he assured his public that Western troops would remain only until the end of the crisis, departing immediately thereafter. Second, his speeches always mentioned the Muslim and Arab troops of the "coalition" before those of the West, thereby implying the primacy of their role. Third, he secured a *fatwa* from the highest fundamentalist Wahhabi authority in Saudi Arabia, Sheikh Bin Baz, and another from the council of senior clergy, sanctioning the presence of the Western troops. A third *fatwa* sanctioning the use of force against the Iraqi army was obtained later.[23] President Mubarak of Egypt also secured a similar *fatwa* from al-Azhar, the highest academy of Sunni Islam in the world.

The response of the Islamic movements themselves, however, was neither uniform nor consistent, particularly at the beginning of the crisis. As events unfolded, most of the movements denounced the use of Western troops to fight the Iraqi Muslim army, although none openly condoned Iraq's occupation of Kuwait. In the streets, the widespread opposition to the presence of Western troops intensified when the shooting began. In those countries—Yemen, Algeria, Morocco, Sudan, Jordan, and Libya—that permitted its expression, such opposition was highly visible; in other countries, notably Egypt, protests were firmly controlled.

Outside of the Gulf states, Islamic movements have remained strong throughout the Arab region in the aftermath of the Gulf War. Besides enduring immense economic burdens, large sectors of the Arab populations, as well as members of the governments that supported the war, experienced disappointment and frustration as the feeling grew that the Arabs as a whole had been defeated[24] in a war initiated by Saddam and exploited by the Western powers to their own advantage. This, coupled with the demise of pan-Arabism and socialism, has led increasing numbers of Arabs to give their support to various forms of Islamism. Active and ready to lure new members and supporters, Islamic movements are seizing the opportunity to expand their ranks, particularly among the young.

THE STATUS OF ISLAMIC MOVEMENTS

The nature of Islamic movements varies, depending on the social and political contexts in which they operate. For example, significant differences exist between the political strategies, goals, and even doctrinal tenets of Shi'i Islam, which prevails in Iran and parts of Lebanon, and those of Sunni Islam, which predominates among Arabs. The Muslim Brotherhood in Syria differs in its political means and goals from its counterparts in Egypt, Jordan, and Lebanon[25] and also from such militant Islamic groups as Islamic Jihad and Muhammad's Army. Given this diversity, as well as the lack of reliable information concerning the organization and activities of underground movements such as the Shiite Islamic groups in Iraq,[26] it is unhelpful to generalize across the Arab world. A wiser approach is to examine the present status of Islamism in selected Arab states, thereby conveying the diversity of Islamism while also indicating certain characteristics common to all of the movements and pointing to possible future developments in other parts of the Arab world. Of the six countries that form the focus of this book, three—Egypt, Jordan, and Algeria—possess visible and influential Islamic movements.

Egypt

Egyptian society is overwhelmingly Muslim, with Islamic values constituting a major component of all populist ideologies, including Nasserism, which, despite its secular orientation, was never antagonistic toward Islam. Nasser's long standing dispute with the Muslim Brotherhood concerned not Islam, but rather the use of violence to topple an Egyptian regime headed by a "devout" Muslim. During his first years in power, Sadat encouraged the rise of political Islam, cracking down only when it began to constitute a serious threat to his regime. In the wake of Sadat's assassination by a militant Islamic group, Mubarak adopted a two-pronged strategy: to be conciliatory toward mainstream Islamic groups such as the Brethren while being firm against the small, armed groups that advocate violent means for the achievement of their political goals.

The demise of socialist pan-Arabism has further strengthened Islamism, and ever-increasing numbers of Egyptians are responding to calls for the Islamization of society or the implementation of the *shari'a*. Well aware of the popular appeal of such demands, the government has adopted some measures designed to please devout Muslims. The sale of alcohol has been prohibited in 14 out of 26 governorates,[27] and there has been an increase in the number of television programs featuring such outspoken fundamentalist speakers as Sheikh Muhammad Mutawalli al-Sha'rawi, who appears regularly on state-run Egyptian television responding to queries about the position of Islam toward many social and political issues.

The Islamization of Egyptian society also has a darker side. The Jihad, founded by the blind cleric Sheikh Omar Abdul Rahman,[28] was accused of gunning down Rif'at al-Mahgoub, the speaker of the National Assembly, during the 1990 Gulf crisis. Other smaller groups, employing violence against both the state and the Copts are also beginning to emerge. Having accused Abdul Rahman of collaborating with the authorities, one of these, the Shawqiyeen (followers of Sheikh Shawqi from Fayyoum in Upper Egypt), has launched attacks on the Egyptian police. Armed bands have also targeted churches, Copt-owned businesses, foreign tourists, and Muslims who refuse to submit to them,[29] or those, such as the writer Farag Foda,[30] who have publicly condemned their actions.

The religious resurgence has not been limited to Islam. Influenced by the current international trend toward revival of ethnic and religious identities, as well as by the sectarian dimension of the civil war in Lebanon, which some local and Western media have depicted as a war against Christian Arabs, Copts have also begun to display their religious identity and loyalty more visibly. Many observe religious rituals more regularly, celebrate religious holidays with more fanfare, and wear large crosses around their necks. Thus it appears that religious fundamentalism—and its inherent tendency toward intolerance and away from compromise—is becoming a powerful force in both communities, a situation that is unlikely to change, even if economic conditions were to improve substantially.

Thus far, Mubarak has sought to contain this potentially explosive situation by making concessions to moderate Islamists and conservative traditionalists, whose views probably reflect the beliefs of most Egyptians, in the hope of driving a wedge between them and militant extremists. For example, the Muslim Brethren are allowed freedom of expression through their daily paper and other publications. They are also permitted to engage in social activities, such as running health centers, social welfare institutions, and schools, and to preach and lead prayers in mosques and cultural centers. Nevertheless, their organization remains officially illegal because Egyptian law prohibits the establishment of political parties on the basis of religion.

At the same time, however, there is evidence that government concessions to traditional elements have begun to impinge on the free expression of more liberal points of view. For example, the 1991 publication of a work of fiction considered "blasphemous"[31] by an Islamic research agency connected with the Azhar[32] resulted in a sentence of several years imprisonment for its author Ala' Hamed and his publisher. In January 1992, five books of a noted Islamic liberal, Muhammad Sa'id Ashmawy, chief judge of the Higher State Security Court, along with a book on the Jihad organization by the journalist Adel Hammouda, were confiscated from the Cairo International Book Exhibit by the same research agency. President Mubarak himself was forced to intervene and order the books returned to the exhibit.

While attempting to accommodate the more moderate traditional elements, the government has cracked down on militant Islamists, arresting and jailing many of them. In March 1992, the holy month of Ramadan, Mubarak publicly denounced "negative trends" in the Islamic world that deviate from "the essence of the Koran and the teachings of Islam." He described this phenomenon as "sickness" that needed to be "decisively cured and boldly confronted" by combating "sectarian discord, doctrinal extremism, intellectual terrorism, the exploitation of religion."

Although Mubarak noted that Islam calls for tolerance and freedom of belief,[33] his speech followed a number of publicized and unpublicized clashes between Muslim fundamentalist youth, on the one hand, and Copts, government security forces, and other Islamic groups, on the other. The authorities blamed the Jihad group led by Abdul Rahman for these incidents. A particularly significant Muslim-Christian encounter occurred in September 1991 in the Cairo district of Imbaba when hundreds of Muslim militants took to the streets, defacing portraits of the Virgin Mary and burning Christian-owned shops.[34] These clashes marked the extension of religious conflict from southern Egypt to Cairo, a city that has rarely witnessed such incidents in its modern history. The social composition of Imbaba makes it a likely site for further religious conflicts. It is an impoverished, congested slum whose residents firmly adhere to religion in its most constrictive, rigid strain.

In May 1992 a second, more violent sectarian battle took place in Minshiyat Nasser in the governorate of Assyut in Upper Egypt, an area where village and clan feuds are common. This battle resulted in the death of a dozen Christians and one of the Muslim assailants,[35] prompting President Mubarak to travel to the troubled area in an effort to soothe the aggrieved and reconcile Muslim-Christian differences. The Egyptian Organization for Human Rights attributed the armed assault to a dispute over payments demanded by the Islamic group, which has imposed its own laws, exacted taxes from businesses,[36] and barred Christians from expressing their religious beliefs in public.[37]

These clashes, based on misperceptions and unfounded information, reflected the growing distrust between Copts and a large segment of Muslims. One fundamentalist leader in Imbaba has publicly asserted the belief that, having succeeded in gaining control of vital areas of business such as gold shops, the Christians are conspiring to take over all of Egypt.[38] Even many nonfundamentalist Muslims criticize the Copts for blocking the adoption of the *shari'a* in Egypt, describing their act as "the tyranny of the minority."[39] For their part, Christian elites blamed the government for failing to respond to the grievances of 6 million Copts[40] by "selling more Islam" rather than advocating secularism and democracy.[41] Coptic associations in the West accused the Egyptian government of condoning an anti-

Christian campaign, calling on the international community to step in and "help to save the Copts from further destruction."[42]

The Assyut incident cannot be dismissed as a clan or village feud, nor can it be attributed solely to "unemployment among youths,"[43] as some analysts have argued in the case of Imbaba clashes. Neither a pure rebellion of the dispossessed and repressed, nor a religious war, nor a "conspiracy" by the regime and the fundamentalists to destroy the Copts, the Assyut incident is part of a multifaceted conflict with religious, class, and antiestablishment dimensions. Its participants are poor, politically repressed, religious fundamentalists determined to Islamize their society by force, beginning in their immediate community. Having failed to overthrow the central government, they have subsequently directed their frustration against more accessible targets: first the Christians, then Western tourists who, in their view, are protected by the "un-Islamic" regime and share religious beliefs with another enemy, the West.[44] Another objective of attacking tourists is to weaken the country's economy by pushing domestic investment away from tourism. It appears that the tradition of religious toleration that flourished in Egypt for centuries is now being challenged by strong Islamic fundamentalist forces and by Christian assertions of a distinct identity. As intolerance and mutual distrust between Muslims and Christians in mixed neighborhoods grow, the extremists in both communities can easily incite violence, which is likely to become even more bloody and atrocious.

Yet, there are three factors that strongly militate against the possibility that Egypt will reach the extent of strife that prevailed in Lebanon in the 1970s and 1980s. First, the Egyptian tradition of religious toleration is centuries old and deeply rooted, serving as a guiding principle for both traditional, conservative Muslim groups and institutions, notably the Azhar, and mainstream Islamic movements, such as the Muslim Brotherhood, which has adopted peaceful means of achieving its political goals. Second, the Egyptian state is composed of long-standing, stable institutions that are highly resistant to radical, extremist politics. The stability of these institutions is further reinforced by state domination of social and economic activities, which renders a large segment of the population directly dependent upon them.[45] Third, the regular army and security forces have so far proven to be united, nonsectarian, and effective, moving swiftly to end sectarian clashes and to combat armed bands of extremists. Only in the unlikely event of a large-scale infiltration of the army by Islamic militants would there be a real threat to the stability of the regime.

Nevertheless, given the power of Islamic values and the popular appeal of the call for the implementation of the *shari'a*, Egypt will probably become a more Islamized, national territorial state. While striving to maintain tolerance of other beliefs, the regime may be confronted with irresistible popular pressure to widen the application of measures that are considered consistent with the *shari'a* and to restrict or abandon others that are inconsistent with it. Although such steps could undermine the power of political extremists by depriving them of their ideological base, they may also further alienate the Christian minority.

Jordan

The Jordanian regime was taken by surprise by the 1989 elections,[46] in which Islamists won 34 out of 80 parliamentary seats. Twenty-two of these seats were won by the mainstream Muslim Brotherhood, an organization that was relatively unaffected by the ban on political parties because its official status was that of a charitable organization. Alarmed by the prospect of a division of the country along religious lines, the king initially resisted the Brotherhood's attempts to be represented in the cabinet. However, as the Islamists garnered even more popular support because of their antiwar stance during the Gulf crisis, cooperation between the Islamists and the regime increased and members of the Brotherhood were appointed to cabinet positions in January 1991.[47]

Despite its control of important cabinet portfolios, the Brotherhood encountered stiff opposition from the secular community when its ministers and members of parliament (MPs) tried to outlaw the manufacture, sale, and consumption of alcohol, segregate the sexes in the workplace, and ban fathers from observing their daughters' participation in school sports. With the tacit support of the king, secular MPs and ministers resisted these demands, forcing the fundamentalists to back down on most of them. The secular counter-offensive was further strengthened by the king's approval of a National Charter signed by the Muslim Brotherhood and other political parties. (The Brotherhood, it should be explained, had to sign the charter to maintain its legality as a political party.) While declaring the *shari'a* to be the source of law in the country,[48] the charter, which provides for personal freedom, freedom of expression and organization, and a multiparty system, clearly circumscribes the power of the Islamic movement. The Islamists suffered another major setback in June 1991, when the king, preparing to join the Middle East peace process, dismissed the cabinet and appointed as prime minister Taher al-Masri, a Palestinian who supports a negotiated settlement with Israel.

Opposition to the Madrid peace talks ended the Brotherhood's alliance with the crown. To gather support for its position, the Brotherhood called for a public rally on October 11, 1991. This effort was blocked when the cabinet banned the rally and the Brotherhood was forced to back away from a head-on confrontation with the regime. Later in the month, the Brotherhood joined other pan-Arab parties in an indoor rally that attracted approximately 1,000 people: It was disbanded by police following a clash between pro- and anti-Madrid groups.[49] In a subsequent gathering of some 4,000 fundamentalists at Amman's principal mosque, a Brotherhood speaker denounced the Madrid conference, calling for a *jihad* to liberate all of Palestine. At the same time, however, he clearly stated that his party would express its opposition to the Jordanian position without resorting to violence,[50] thereby revealing that although the Islamists were ideologically opposed to a peace settlement with Israel under the terms of UN Resolution 242, they did not want a showdown with the government over the Madrid talks.

In October 1991, Brotherhood opponents of the policies of the Masri government were joined by members of the proestablishment Constitutional Bloc, following that party's exclusion from a reshuffled cabinet. With preparations for the Madrid peace conference at a crucial stage, these two groups together mustered a majority (49) of MPs who signed a petition calling for Masri's resignation. Reacting to the disorder in his house, King Hussein sought to mobilize popular support for the decision to join the peace talks by convening a national congress on October 12, 1991. Some 2,500 influential Jordanians, including MPs, senators, former premiers and ministers, heads of professional associations, mayors, and other elected officials attended; the Muslim Brotherhood, however, chose to boycott the congress. In an effort to convince Jordanians of the soundness of his decision, the monarch responded to various concerns and questions raised by the opposition by explaining that "we must be involved in the drive for peace because it concerns our present and future and has an impact on our continuity."[51]

The following month, King Hussein replaced Masri, appointing a Hashemite Sharif of the royal family, Zayd Bin Shaker, prime minister. Bin Shaker is a capable, veteran politician of good reputation who cannot be attacked by MPs with impunity. One MP aptly described him as "a man who is always powerful, whether or not he is in office. Deputies who know better will not forget that."[52] As expected, Bin Shaker initially adopted a tougher stance against the anti-Madrid parties, while maintaining the general political and economic policies of his predecessor by retaining the ministers of foreign affairs, finance, and interior. Reports claim that he threatened the Islamists with a dissolution of parliament and early elections in which they would not be assured of victory (opinion polls were revealing a dramatic decline in popular support for the Brotherhood).[53] Ultimately, however, the new premier struck a deal with the Islamists, allowing them to retain the speakership of parliament in exchange for a vote of confidence in the cabinet.

The policy of the new government was guided by statements the king made in his letter of appointment to Bin Shaker and in a speech to the senate and the lower house. In his letter, the king implied that Masri's MP critics had overstepped their authority, and he denounced the so-called "intellectual terrorism" that violated "democracy and the principles of the National Charter."[54] His speech emphasized the role of parliamentarians in "preserving the authority of the state and its various institutions." In a clear reference to the fundamentalists' rigid views and attempt to dictate government policy, the king said:

> Democracy does not confer on any single group a claim of monopoly over wisdom or truth. Nor does it provide a license to justify encroachment on the rights and liberties of the vast majority of the people. . . .
> Preaching and guidance are closely associated with maintaining national unity, enhancing the forces of amity and solidarity and promoting the general good in a climate that does not allow for bigotry, intolerance, or introversion. This being the case, we would emphasize that the principal role of mosques and other places of worship is to educate people in matters of religion, urge them towards virtue, integrity, respect for public order and a firm rejection of division or disarray among the citizens.[55]

Meanwhile, the authorities clamped down on members of a clandestine, militant Islamic group known as Prophet Muhammad's Army, accusing them of planting bombs, setting fire to a liquor store, attacking a foreign bank, and plotting to overthrow the government. Of the 18 arrested and tried, 8 were sentenced to death. These sentences created an uproar among Islamists both in Jordan and Egypt, resulting in appeals to the monarch for commutations. They were also criticized by Amnesty International, which cited evidence that testimony was obtained from some of the defendants under torture. The king responded by commuting the sentences of six to life imprisonment, but retaining those of the two who were tried in absentia.[56]

To date, King Hussein has introduced some democratic measures, while preventing any group from claiming a monopoly over Islamic interpretation. In stark contrast to Egypt, the new Jordanian law on political parties does not ban parties based on religion; however, it does require them to formulate a specific platform[57] beyond the implementation of the *shari'a*. Jordanian politics encompass a vast array of factions and groups, most of which are not political parties in the Western sense. These groups tend to coalesce into two major, rival blocs, Islamic and secular.[58] In the future, it seems the emerging Islamist coalition will be formed around the Muslim Brotherhood, while the secular coalition will be heavily influenced by the king and may lack a single leading party. Neither will be openly antiestablishment.

In May 1992, Islamists suffered a serious electoral reversal in Irbid, Jordan's second largest city, where the "reformist bloc" won 11 of the 12 seats on Irbid city council, a body that had been dominated by the Islamists for the past 12 years. Reflecting on the outcome, a senior government official noted that, despite its organizational strength and elaborate network of social relationships,[59] the Muslim Brotherhood was unable to convince the electorate of the worth of its "Islamic alternative." In late May, the Association of Workers in Land Transport and Mechanics, the largest labor union in Jordan with a membership of 107,000 workers, elected a new 77-member administrative committee. The new leadership was described as mostly "liberal with centrist political views." Only in the city of Zarqa did Muslim Brotherhood candidates win.[60]

The Islamists experienced a setback when two of their elected MPs, Ya'qub al-Qarsh and Laith Shbeilat, were arrested on charges of stockpiling unlicensed weapons, sponsoring a secret, terrorist group, and conspiring against the state. The charges and subsequent conviction in court raised doubts about the Islamists' present and future loyalty to the throne. After demonstrating the power and vigilance of his regime and its firm policy toward any subversive activity, the king pardoned the sentenced MPs, who had pledged their support to him and who had claimed that the arms they stored were to be used against Israel rather than the kingdom.

Nevertheless, the outcome of the struggle for power between the Islamists and a heterogeneous array of secular nationalists, both territorial and pan-Arab, is not yet certain; two factors—the fate of the Middle East peace talks and the state of the economy—are likely to have a significant impact. The necessity of concluding a peace agreement with Israel was reinforced by the influx of some 300,000 Palestinians from the Gulf states. If the peace process fails to produce tangible results within the next couple of years, the Islamic movement will have a good opportunity to impose its vision on the government. At the same time, signs of further deterioration in the economy and large-scale corruption and mismanagement in state institutions are likely to fuel frustration and dissent, particularly among the youth.

Because Islamist symbolism remains appealing to many Jordanian Muslims, the fact that King Hussein, a Hashemite, is a descendent of the Prophet Muhammad endows him with an exceptional legitimacy that is coveted by all other Arab leaders, notably the Saudi monarchs. The king has capitalized on this hereditary asset in the past and will undoubtedly use it in the future to gain leverage over the Islamists. Nevertheless, he may be forced to make further concessions, as President Mubarak has done, in order to stem the tide of fundamentalism. Thus far, King Hussein has proven himself to be one of the shrewdest, most open-minded Arab leaders in contemporary history, as well as the longest surviving monarch in the region. For the foreseeable future, his rule guarantees the country's stability and its ability to be flexible and realistic in peace talks with Israel. In the event of King Hussein's sudden death or resignation due to illness, his successor (whether Crown Prince Hassan or his son, Prince Ali) is unlikely to deviate significantly from the regime's present policies, although Prince Hassan is known to be less sympathetic toward the Palestinians.

Algeria

The Islamic movement in Algeria began to emerge following the introduction of democratic measures in February 1989. Prior to the January 1992 crackdown, four Islamic parties played major roles: the Islamic Salvation Front (FIS), the Movement for an Islamic Society (HAMAS), the Movement of the Islamic Renaissance (MNI), and the Movement for Democracy in Algeria (MDA). The FIS, whose ultimate goal is the Islamization of society through control of political power by any available means, was the largest and most popular party at the time. HAMAS, founded in 1990 by Sheikh Nahnah, supports the principle of political pluralism. The MNI of Sheikh Djaballah shares the views of the mainstream Muslim Brotherhood of Egypt and Jordan in all aspects except economic liberalization, to which it is opposed.[61] The MDA, led by former President Ben Bella, advocates a reformist version of Islam.

In contrast to the situation prevailing in the Arab East (Mashriq), Islamism in Algeria and the Maghreb has generally not been a rival ideology to pan-Arabism. Given the virtual absence of local Christians within an overwhelmingly Sunni population and the presence of large numbers of non-Arab Berbers, Islam has played a unifying role,[62] and Arabic has become a "sacred" language. The secular line of demarcation between pan-Arabism and Islamism has little significance for Maghrebi pan-Arabs. Algerian Islamism, unlike that of Saudi Arabia, has been radical and populist, despite having been financed for a number of years by Saudi largesse.

Since the early days of Algerian independence in 1962, the FLN had enjoyed a monopoly on power. Over those decades, the incompetence and corruption of its leadership had brought Algeria, a country rich in oil, gas, and gold, to the brink of economic ruin.[63] In June 1990, the Islamists won a landslide victory in municipal and provincial elections, thereby discrediting the FLN. The FLN fought its defeat by attempting to gerrymander electoral districts in order to minimize Islamist representation in the new assembly. The FIS responded by holding street protests that forced the president to remove Prime Minister Mouloud Hamroche. His successor, Sid Ahmad Ghozali, came to office with a promise to revise the electoral law and to hold fair elections.

Having grown intolerant of the rising Islamist challenge to the ruling party, in June 1991 top army commanders set out to reassert state authority. They began by attempting to replace Islamist slogans in town halls with the FLN motto, but these efforts were firmly resisted by FIS militants. The army then arrested two of the principal FIS leaders, Abbasi Madany and Ali Belhaj, charging them with conspiracy against the state. During the same month, some 2,500 FIS members and supporters were also arrested.[64] The FLN leadership hoped that bans on political speeches and meetings in mosques, combined with mass arrests intended to deprive the FIS of its leadership and active cadres, would liquidate the opposition. Many Arab journalists and politicians believed this was possible as, in their view, the Islamist "phenomenon" was on the wane because it had supported Saddam during the Gulf War. An Egyptian journalist, writing one month before the Algerian national elections, predicted that the fundamentalist movement in all Arab countries "could soon be finished as a major force on the political street."[65]

To the surprise of many analysts, the FIS won the first round of elections in November 1991, garnering 81 percent of the seats, an outcome that stunned not only the Algerian leadership but also that of the rest of the Arab world. Immediately following the elections, over 100,000 people took to the streets of Algiers, demonstrating in support of democracy. While Anis Mansour, an Egyptian journalist known to be a confidant of President Mubarak, expressed exaggerated alarm, predicting that Islamist control might ultimately extend from Tunisia to Syria,[66] other analysts urged President Benjedid to stand up and refuse to deliver his country to a new totalitarianism, and offered advice on how to "clip the claws" of the FIS.[67]

On January 12, 1992, a few days before the second ballot, the Algerian army took control, forcing President Benjedid to resign. The High Committee of State (HCS), a new five-man governing body headed by the revolutionary leader Muhammad Boudiaf, was created. Reaction in the Arab world was mixed. While some observers felt army intervention was justified, others were outraged at the abrogation of democracy. Western and Arab regimes, with the exception of that of Sudan, were generally relieved, and the government of neighboring Tunisia openly rejoiced as it prepared for the trials of its own outlawed Islamists.

Meanwhile, the Algerian leadership attempted to eliminate the FIS through the enactment of laws and decrees. Affirming its commitment to democracy and promising to hold parliamentary and presidential elections within two years, the new government, headed by former Prime Minister Ghozali, declared a state of emergency and banned religious and linguistic-based parties.[68] In response, the FIS went underground, appointing a new secret leadership made up of unknowns.[69] Most opposition parties, including the other Islamist parties, rejected the cancellation of elections and the dissolution of the FIS. Sheikh Nahnah of the Algerian HAMAS warned of more violence if the authorities continued to reject negotiations with the Islamists.

The FIS, or radical groups within its ranks, have employed a variety of tactics in their battle with security forces, ranging from armed resistance to the implementation of government decisions, to bombings and the assassination of police officers. One clash took place as a result of the rejection of the appointment of a proestablishment imam to one of the mosques. Another, more serious, confrontation between armed fundamentalists and the army occurred in the mountains near Algiers in late May 1992, resulting in 150 arrests. By the end of May 1992, an estimated 8,000 FIS members and supporters[70] were held without charge in prison camps in the desert where the temperature in the summer exceeds 45 degrees Celsius. The FIS maintained that the number was higher, and accused the government of torturing the detainees and deliberately over-crowding the desert prisons. In an attempt to reduce the tension with the FIS, Boudiaf released about half of the prisoners a few days before his assassination on June 29, 1992.[71]

Reports just prior to Boudiaf's death indicated that Algerian lead-ers had begun to believe that support for the FIS would decline as a result of the jailing of thousands of militants.[72] Many citizens and analysts, however, did not share this belief, citing the fact that, despite the merciless government crackdown, the FIS continued to produce a newsletter and official communiqués and to launch lim-ited attacks on the government.[73] In addition, the FIS won a larger electoral victory in 1991 than in 1990, an indication that popular support was undiminished by the jailing of the principal leaders and approximately 2,500 party cadres.

This support is based on factors other than the FIS's uncertain role in killing Boudiaf.[74] One of the principal factors is the eco-nomic crisis, which was largely created by the incompetent and corrupt bureaucracy of the ruling party. High levels of unemploy-ment, particularly among the young, combined with widespread political repression, are not conducive to stability or public support for the regime. In addition, as a result of its suppression, the FIS may have gained increased legitimacy, both domestically and among international prodemocracy forces. By contrast, the HCS, which was imposed by the army, lacks legitimacy among most Algerians and Algerian parties.

Thus, the young Islamist movement in Algeria may continue to be a powerful political force in the coming years. However, given the failure of the FIS to gain power through peaceful means, it is likely that the party will be dominated by radical, militant elements, thereby increasing the probability of protracted conflict between fundamentalists and other groups led by the army and secular politicians.

CONCLUSION

In the last 50 years, the Arab world has been profoundly influenced by three distinct ideologies: socialist pan-Arabism, Islamism, and territorial nationalism. Growing in strength during the 1940s, social-ist pan-Arabism reached its zenith in the 1950s and continued to enjoy considerable popularity through the mid-1970s, despite severe setbacks in 1961, 1967, and 1971. Since the Camp David Accords were signed in 1978, however, socialist pan-Arabism has been in steady decline. Its demise allowed territorial nationalism (*qutriyya* or *wataniyya*) and Islamism to sweep across the Arab world. The first was openly endorsed by most Arab states and implicitly adopted by almost all, while the second became the ideology of popular dissent among the unemployed, the alienated, the frustrated, and the repressed. By capitalizing on the failures of Arab regimes before, during, and after the Gulf War, Islamic groups have expanded their popular clientele.

Arabs regimes have adopted a two-pronged policy toward Islamists, being more conciliatory toward the mainstream, nonviolent groups such as the Muslim Brotherhood, and cracking down on the small armed groups that advocate violence as a means to establish Islamic states. The ruling elites have made concessions to moderate Islamists and conservative traditionalists in the hope of gaining their support in the raging war against militant fundamentalists. However, these concessions could turn the authoritarian Arab regimes into more Islamized, national territorial states in which non-Muslim minorities are further alienated.

Today, more than two years after the end of the Gulf War, the outcome of the struggle for power between the Islamists and a heterogeneous array of secular nationalists led by the ruling elites is far from certain. Which side will emerge victorious will depend largely on three factors: the fate of the Middle East peace talks, the state of each country's economy, and the prospects for democratization within each nation.

five

The Atomization of the
Arab Regional System

႙႟ In earlier chapters, the Arab world has been depicted as
culturally cohesive, yet rich in socioeconomic and political diversity. This tension between collective and conflicting interests has profoundly influenced attempts to organize regional cooperation since World War II. On the one hand, the League of Arab States was inspired by the belief that the Arab states had enough in common to form a united Arab front able to defend and advance the region's interests within the international community. On the other hand, however, the centrifugal force of diversity among states has proved no less powerful than the centripetal force generated by their shared concerns. The practical consequences of this contradiction are periods of regional solidarity alternating with years of disarray.

The effect of the Gulf War has been to shift the balance firmly in the direction of disarray. During the two years since the end of the Gulf War, Arab politics have become more atomized, with each state placing its domestic interests ahead of regional or subregional interests and thereby undermining any hope of making organizations such as the Arab League and the Arab Maghreb Union effective instruments of a collective Arab policy.

This process of atomization has been accentuated by the ever-present lack of trust among Arab political leaders. Groups and states other than one's family, tribe, or religious or residential community are not easily trusted. As the U.S. sociologist Morroe Berger, has observed:

Cooperation in the Near East is not a conscious effort of distinct groups
to come together for mutual benefit, but simply the result of each
individual playing his part as a member of his family or other group.[1]

Even within a single country, real cooperation is usually restricted
to parochial groups. In Egyptian villages, for example, the writer and
cleric Father Henry Ayrout found that social groups are composed
of a set of independent units that abhor cooperation between
groups, forming "a mass" rather than "an organism."[2] Arabs are still
influenced by the medieval tribal principles of equality and justice.
For them, justice is collective because responsibility rests with the
group rather than the individual. An innocent member of a perpe-
trator's tribe or clan can be held responsible for the tribe's wrong-
doing. Although Islam's prohibition on collective punishment has
reduced the frequency and intensity of bloody feuds and retaliation, it has by no means eliminated the practice.

This chapter first describes the broad course of the Arab regional
system from 1945 to 1990 and the Arab response to the Gulf crisis,
and it then explores in detail how intraregional relations have
changed in the aftermath of the war. As will be seen, hostility
between states and groups of states within the Arab world has
greatly increased, and once-dormant disputes have revived with
alarming vigor. Few if any Arab countries have emerged stronger
from the Gulf War; even leading Arab members of the anti-Iraq
coalition have discovered that, far from their achieving greater security and independence of action at the expense of Iraq, they have
only become more dependent on extraregional powers, particularly
the United States.

THE ARAB REGIONAL SYSTEM: 1945–1990

Since 1945 the Arab system has passed through several phases of
development. The first phase covered the 20 or so years preceding
the 1967 Arab-Israeli war. During this time, most Arab countries
attained political independence from Europe. However, the sovereignty of some of the new entities was not recognized by others,
which either intervened directly in the domestic affairs of their
neighbors, such as Egypt and Saudi Arabia in Yemen, or made territorial claims, such as Iraq's claim to Kuwait. The result was what the
late president of the American University of Beirut, Malcolm Kerr,
called "the Arab cold war."[3]

The second phase occurred between 1967 and 1974, when the
Arab states gained increasing legitimacy with respect to their sister

states, as manifested in the sharp decline in interstate intervention. The limited, unsuccessful military intervention by Syria in Jordan's domestic war against the PLO in 1970 was a noteworthy exception to the newfound atmosphere of consensus and solidarity. During this period, Nasser initiated summit meetings of Arab heads of state as a more effective forum for coordinating regional policies than the regular meetings of the Arab League. This interstate cooperation culminated in the 1973 Egyptian-Syrian military offensive against Israel and the subsequent cutoff of Arab oil shipments to the West. At the same time, the PLO was recognized as the sole representative of the Palestinian people, an act that enabled that organization to play a far more significant role in regional politics.[4]

The third phase of the development of the Arab system lasted from 1975 to 1978, during which time Arab solidarity declined, reaching its nadir in 1978 with the signing of the Camp David Accords. The Egyptian government was sharply criticized for making a unilateral decision that could impinge on the security of other Arab states and weaken collective Arab efforts to regain the occupied territories and establish a Palestinian state. Egypt was evicted from the Arab League, which subsequently relocated its headquarters to Tunis, and was shunned by most Arab governments well into the 1980s. Efforts to reintegrate Egypt into the Arab community began during the Iran-Iraq War, since Egyptian military and political support was needed to counter Iranian aggression. As the Iraqi position worsened, a few Arab countries, notably Iraq itself as well as Jordan and Saudi Arabia, reached out to Egypt, albeit often in an unpublicized fashion.

The fourth and latest phase of Arab interstate relations has been marked by disarray within the Arab regional order and the growing irrelevance of Arabism to state policies, as reflected in the lack of any effective Arab opposition to the 1982 Israeli incursion into Lebanon and in the persistence of the Lebanese civil war, which was fueled by some Arab states. The Arab League, which once stood for Arab cooperation and solidarity, was greatly weakened as its members began to group themselves into rival blocs. Secret terrorist warfare and official media wars erupted between Syria and Iraq, Egypt and Libya, Morocco and Algeria, and Syria and the PLO.

At the same time, however, some efforts were made to establish regional cooperation. In an effort to counter the escalation of the Iran-Iraq War, the five Gulf states were prompted by Saudi Arabia to establish the Gulf Cooperation Council (GCC) in 1981. The Maghreb countries—Algeria, Morocco, Tunisia, Libya, and Mauritania—

created their own bloc, the Arab Maghreb Union, in 1989, partly in response to domestic pressure for political change. Egypt, Iraq, Jordan, and Yemen followed suit, forming the Arab Cooperation Council in the same year.

On the eve of the Gulf crisis, four states—Egypt, Saudi Arabia, Iraq, and Syria—played critical roles in Arab regional politics. Egypt, which had been readmitted to the Arab League, was attempting to regain its former status as leader of the Arab world. Although no longer the preeminent military power in the Arab world, it remained a key actor because of its size, its human resources, and its strong relationship with the West engendered by the Camp David Accords. Saudi Arabia was the financier, providing poorer states with major development loans and funds for arms purchases. It was also the chief mediator of disagreements among Arabs. Although the Saudi approach to dispute settlement was usually timid, awaiting the moment when mediation efforts were sure to succeed, it used its economic power to win or strengthen friendships, bribe rivals and opponents, and sweeten settlement deals between feuding "brothers" in the region. Capitalizing on its strategic location, Iraq rose to prominence following the isolation of Egypt and the oil price increases of the mid-1970s. It gained additional military and political importance in its war with Iran, during which the Iraqi forces expanded and acquired advanced weaponry. Syria, the arch-enemy of the Iraqi regime and the most trusted Arab ally of Iran,[5] was the only Arab state whose military buildup could pose a direct threat to Israel.

Algeria and Morocco also played important roles in regional politics, participating in efforts to reconcile differences between Arab states and between Arabs and the West.[6] For example, in concert with Saudi Arabia, Algeria and Morocco succeeded in getting the major warring factions in Lebanon to end the country's protracted strife and endorse a letter of national accord in 1989.

THE RESPONSE OF ARAB STATES TO THE GULF CRISIS

Stunned by the Iraqi invasion of Kuwait on August 2, 1990, the Arab states were slower than the West, particularly Britain and the United States, to comprehend the significance of Saddam Hussein's move. In addition, they failed to agree on a unified plan of action. Some states and political groups, notably Jordan and the PLO, acted unilaterally to try to defuse the crisis but were unable to convince Saddam Hussein to withdraw his troops unconditionally. Arab mediation efforts were interrupted when a majority of Arab League members denounced Iraq's action and supported the deployment of foreign troops to defend Saudi territory. Although none of the Arab states condoned Iraq's aggression, a significant number opposed the presence of Western forces in the Gulf, in effect siding with Iraq during Operation Desert Shield/Storm.

The Gulf states, supported by Egypt and Syria, formed the core of the Arab-Western alliance against Saddam. Jordan, the PLO, Yemen, Sudan, Libya, and Algeria constituted the core of the opposition, rejecting the use of foreign forces and favoring instead Arab efforts to resolve the Iraq-Kuwait conflict peacefully. While tolerating domestic expression of pro-Iraqi sentiments, Morocco sent a symbolic contingent to Saudi Arabia. Tunisia followed a similar policy without sending any troops. Meanwhile, the stance of the pro-Iraqi contingent was essentially political. Although Jordan provided some financial support to Iraq, largely to ensure its own economic survival, no Arab state allowed its territory to be used as a staging ground for attacks against coalition forces.

The shifts in political alignments resulting from the Gulf crisis led to the collapse or the marginalization of the roles of blocs. The Arab Cooperation Council, formed in 1989 by Egypt, Iraq, Jordan, and Yemen, ceased to exist as Egypt and Iraq became enemies and the remaining members opposed the Gulf War. The bloc of Maghrebi states played no significant role, although substantial numbers of Maghrebis supported Saddam's challenge to the West.[7] The GCC had only symbolic value, as none of its members, including Saudi Arabia, was capable of defending itself or its GCC partners.

In the aftermath of Desert Storm, relations among Arab states continue to be heavily influenced by their wartime positions. Kuwaitis and most other "Gulfies" retain vivid memories of the Iraqi atrocities and of support for Saddam among Palestinians and Jordanians. Kuwait and Saudi Arabia, both of which had extended generous financial assistance to Arab states and to their Islamic parties, felt betrayed when Jordan, Yemen, and Sudan, as well as the PLO, failed to support them in the conflict. Influenced by Bedouin traditions, which place a high value on loyalty and group solidarity, Kuwait and Saudi Arabia are now determined to punish these states. Punishment has been collective and vindictive. In some cases, it has even been justified by implausible theories of conspiracy, such as the Saudi belief that King Hussein conspired with Saddam to take over Saudi Arabia, or at least to regain possession of the Hijaz, which was once ruled by his grandfather Sharif Hussein.[8]

The resulting mass expulsions of Palestinians and Jordanians from Kuwait and Yemenis from Saudi Arabia are a source of pervasive and lingering resentment.

Postwar relations between the two major combatants of the Gulf War, Iraq and Kuwait, remain extremely hostile. The regimes are engaged in a propaganda war aimed at demonizing each other in the eyes of their people. In meetings with children of war victims, Saddam Hussein publicly blames Kuwait for the deaths of Iraqi parents and loved ones, while the brutality of the Iraqi occupation of Kuwait has created widespread xenophobia among Kuwaiti citizens toward nonpeninsular Arabs.[9] The Kuwaiti regime and media have not distinguished between the Iraqi regime and its people. They are considered equally vicious and bloodthirsty and therefore deserving of the maximum possible punishment. Ibrahim Shatti, *chef de cabinet* of the Emir of Kuwait, described the Iraqi people as "filled with spite, destructiveness, thuggery, and bloodthirstiness toward the Kuwaiti people—even more so than their leadership." He attributed Iraq's aggression against Kuwait to "a desire for revenge developed among the Iraqi people."[10] Reviewing relations between Iraq and Kuwait over the past 30 years, the former Kuwaiti ambassador to the United States claimed that every Iraqi regime had coveted his country; future regimes, he believed, would have similar designs on Kuwait.[11] This mutual distrust and recrimination is likely to raise the intensity of hostility between Iraqis and Kuwaitis, thereby complicating and prolonging the Iraq-Kuwait dispute for years to come.

A NEW SYSTEM OF DISUNITY

During the two years since the end of the Gulf War, Arab politics have become atomized, with each state explicitly placing its domestic interests before regional or subregional interests. This predominance of national interests over pan-Arab and pan-Islamic concerns is manifested in the malfunctioning of regional and subregional organizations, both private and public. For example, to date, the Arab League has failed to fulfill its mandate to foster cooperation among the Arab states.[12] Regional organizations that survived the war are increasingly incapable of forging joint positions among their members. The Arab Maghreb Union neither convinced Libya, a member state, to comply with the UN resolution on the Lockerbie issue,[13] nor prevented the United States and Britain from convincing the Security Council to enforce sanctions against Libya. It has also failed in its self-assigned mission to reconcile differences between anti-Saddam states and other Arabs. Without Egyptian cooperation and the end of Iraq's isolation by the international community, the Arab Cooperation Council, which was rendered moribund as a result of Egypt's opposition to the Iraqi invasion of Kuwait, has no chance of revival. Even the GCC, ostensibly a more cohesive group, has not been able to resolve bilateral disputes among its members nor to agree on how to deal with Iran and Arab states outside the Gulf region.[14]

This pattern is unlikely to change in the near future, not least because Arab countries lack a civil society. The disorganization or marginalization of domestic social forces prevents pan-Arab agencies from drawing strength from autonomous social and political organizations.[15] The existing Arab regional system has been further weakened by the demise of Iraq as a regional power and by the declining importance of the roles played by other states—notably, Egypt and Saudi Arabia—that were influential in prewar Arab regional politics. Interstate disputes over territories and natural resources have significantly increased, and GCC states are beginning to assert interests that diverge from those of the rest of the Arab world. This situation is further complicated by the activities of non-Arab regional powers such as Israel, Iran, and Turkey, and Western powers, particularly the United States, which have become more involved in Arab regional politics and economics in the aftermath of the Gulf War.

MODIFIED REGIONAL ROLE OF KEY STATES

With the decline of Iraq as a regional power following the Gulf War, three states—Egypt, Saudi Arabia, and Syria—have assumed new roles in Arab affairs. Although the Camp David Accords of 1978 greatly undermined Egypt's position of leadership in the Arab world, by the eve of the Gulf War, President Mubarak had managed to repair a good deal of the damage. These efforts were largely undone, however, by Egyptian support for Western coalition forces during the Gulf War. In this regard, it is worth noting that, during the Arab summit meeting of August 10, 1990, the subject of which was the Iraqi invasion of Kuwait, a group of countries representing slightly less than half of the total Arab population declined to side with the coalition.[16] There is also evidence of disapproval among segments of the populations of states that did support the coalition.[17]

Egypt

The Gulf War brought some economic hardship to Egypt, rendering it more dependent than ever on foreign economic assistance, particularly from the United States. Approximately 1 million Egyptian workers returned from Kuwait and Iraq. Although many of these evacuees may have subsequently replaced the ousted Yemenis in Saudi Arabia or found employment in Libya, the interruption of remittances to their families in Egypt, combined with their personal financial losses, has had an adverse effect on the already strained economy.[18]

Despite recent improvements in the performance of its economy, Egypt's economic vulnerability, together with its much-reduced military power since signing a peace treaty with Israel in 1978, has made other Arab states less willing to accept Egyptian regional leadership. This reluctance is manifested in many ways, both large and small. For example, after signing the Damascus Declaration in March 1991, Saudi Arabia and the Gulf states were reluctant to implement its provisions, which call for an Egyptian security role in return for a generous financial remuneration. Another indication of Egypt's reduced role in the Arab world is the virtual lack of influence it had on Libya with regard to the Lockerbie case, despite the intensive efforts of its diplomats, including President Mubarak and the Egyptian secretary general of the Arab League.

Saudi Arabia

Saudi Arabia formerly financed several regimes and Islamic groups, including Jordan, the PLO, the Jordanian Muslim Brotherhood, and the Algerian FIS.[19] Now, however, it has ceased to do so, realizing that such assistance does not ensure unswerving support for the Saudi position on any given issue. On the contrary, during the Gulf War some of the principal beneficiaries of Saudi largesse stood firmly and openly against the kingdom. This discovery, combined with the economic difficulties resulting from the conflict, led to a transformation of the Saudi Arabian role in the region. Whereas its previous role was that of mediator between conflicting states and groups throughout the Arab world, Saudi Arabia has now become a party to regional conflicts. Saudi relations with its non-GCC Arab neighbors—Iraq, Jordan, and Yemen—which deteriorated during the war, remain strained.

Like the Kuwaitis, the Saudis harbor deep resentment toward Iraq as well as real fear of an Iraqi military revival. The kingdom appears determined to crush Saddam to ensure that he will never threaten Saudi Arabia again. It has shown unprecedented aggressiveness in financing and openly supporting opposition groups in Iraq. GCC statements since the end of the war call for the maintenance of UN sanctions against Iraq, blaming Saddam for all of the civilian misery and deaths in Iraq. The statements seem to assume that the Iraqis, although capable of overthrowing him, have not tried. Relations between Saudi Arabia and other Arab countries have never been characterized by such bitterness, not even during the Nasser era, the previous high point of Saudi-Egyptian rivalry.

Yemen's position during the Gulf War destroyed the long-standing, cordial relationship it previously had enjoyed with Saudi Arabia. Not satisfied with withdrawing the special privileges extended to Yemeni expatriates, the Saudis now seem intent on inflicting more punishment on Yemen. Some Yemenis have accused the Saudis of promoting instability in their recently united country by sponsoring assassinations of Yemeni politicians and their families, and disputes continue over oil exploration rights in the border territory. Yemeni attempts to normalize relations with Saudi Arabia have failed, and mutual distrust lingers.

Relations with Jordan are equally sour, and all Jordanian fence-mending efforts have failed, apparently because of Saudi determination to punish its "disloyal" brother. In a message to King Hussein, delivered through a third party, the Saudis insisted that he publicly apologize for "supporting" Saddam in the Gulf crisis.[20] For King Hussein to do so would constitute an unprecedented public humiliation for an Arab head of state.

As a party to conflicts with three of its Arab neighbors, Saudi Arabia has adopted a more aggressive foreign policy, losing in the process its long-standing role as a neutral third party in inter-Arab disputes. In addition, the policy of restricting economic assistance to trusted allies, subject to strict political and economic conditions, has transformed Saudi Arabia from a major financial force throughout the Arab world into a regional bank that lends limited assistance to a select clientele. At the same time, Saudi Arabia has become much more dependent on the United States for protection from external as well as internal threats.[21]

Syria

The Syrian role in the Arab world has changed in the aftermath of the Gulf War; concerns for its own security have arisen as a result of developments both within the region and beyond. The United States has long considered Syria an international outlaw, an impression that the Syrian government has sought to eliminate.

Although Syria contributed troops to the coalition forces and attempted to win favor with the United States, the American government still considers it to be a sponsor of terrorism[22] and monitors its arms imports closely, a practice that has led to friction between the two countries. Reacting to U.S. attempts to restrict the flow of tanks and missiles to Syria while Israel is allowed to "produce all types of weapons, especially missiles," an angry President Assad lashed out: "That is not international legitimacy. That is the law of the jungle, the law of wild animals. They are trying to impose surrender on us."[23]

The Gulf War eliminated Iraq as a potential threat to Israel and greatly reduced the regional role of Egypt, thereby heightening Syria's domestic security concerns. As Syria is now the only Arab military power that constitutes a threat to Israel, the Syrian government appears concerned that Israel may seek to eliminate this possibility either by means of a preemptive strike against its weapons of mass destruction or by engaging its army in a decisive battle. Given Israeli military superiority, the most likely outcome of such a confrontation would be the neutralization of Syria. This preoccupation with security means that Syria's regional concerns are largely restricted to its local domain,[24] thereby reducing the importance of its wider role in inter-Arab politics. However, it has maintained an important mediating role between Iran and a number of Arab countries. Syria's security concerns also lead it to seek friendly relations—or at least to avoid friction with—the United States, the approval of which Israel needs if it ever decides to launch a major military operation against Syria.

GULF VERSUS NON-GULF STATES

The anti-Saddam coalition, created by the signing of the Damascus Declaration in March 1991, was an unstable alliance from the outset. Great economic and cultural disparities exist between its signatories—Egypt and Syria, on the one hand, and the six GCC states, on the other. The "northern tier," the Mashriq or Levantine states—Egypt, Iraq, Syria, Jordan, and the Palestinians—are proud of their rich cultural heritage and continue to recall the centuries of prosperity they enjoyed while virtually all of the now-GCC territories were poor and primitive. The Mashriq, the land of today's Arab "have-nots," was the home of the great ancient civilizations of Egypt, Sumer, and Babylon. It was also the birthplace of Judaism and Christianity. Islam attained global significance only after it was brought to the Mashriq by the early successors of Prophet Muhammad during the seventh century. Thus, many Levantines find it difficult to accept the sudden change of fortune resulting from the discovery of oil in the Gulf. Lavish spending by peninsular Arabs, as well as their financial support of non-Arab and non-Muslim ventures, often arouse Levantine envy and resentment. For their part, the Gulf regimes have long been aware that most Arabs of the northern tier dislike them for refusing to share what the former perceive as common Arab wealth.[25]

The Damascus agreement provided the poor partners, Egypt and Syria, with a security role in return for which the six wealthy, yet militarily weak, partners offered generous financial remuneration, an arrangement that places the future stability of the GCC countries in jeopardy. At least some pan-Arab ideas derived from Ba'athism and Nasserism remain alive in the ranks of the Egyptian and Syrian armies and could appeal to antiestablishment sectors of the indigenous societies or inspire the guest troops to intervene and tip the delicate domestic balances of power. Furthermore, the presence of Arab forces in the Gulf is not easily defensible from a military standpoint. Unless they come in large numbers with sophisticated weaponry, Egyptian and Syrian forces will not be strong enough to deter a real threat from a regional power like Iraq or Iran. Given their own domestic security needs, Egypt and Syria may not be capable of deploying tens of thousands of highly skilled soldiers for an indefinite period. In addition, a sizable troop deployment could become an occupying army, similar in many ways to Saddam's troops, thereby producing more insecurity than security. This concern was clearly expressed by Kuwaiti authorities, who were worried that large numbers of Egyptian troops could "exacerbate the demographic imbalance" in the emirate and become a source of "future inter-Arab disputes."[26]

Another problem with the Damascus Declaration is the high cost of maintaining a token Arab force at a time of economic decline in the Gulf states and in the world at large.[27] After signing the Damascus Declaration, the GCC states quickly realized the serious economic implications of their act. Their initial pledge of $15 billion in aid to the non-Gulf allies was scaled down to $10 billion then to $6 billion, mainly in the form of loans. Even this reduced sum may never be lent given the strict conditions attached to it.[28]

The Damascus Declaration caused friction with neighboring Iran, which has consistently rejected the idea of entrusting Gulf security to non-Gulf forces. Iran proposed instead a security system restricted to itself, the six GCC states, and, eventually, Iraq. With the defeat of Iraq, however, Iran has become the only regional power with the strength to affect GCC security. It is also the only Shiite state in the world, and thus is a potential magnet for large numbers of Shiites in the GCC countries. Meanwhile, most GCC states have clamored for a greater Iranian role in Gulf security in order to counter the prospect of an Iraqi resurgence. Kuwait, in particular, has been very vocal in this regard. The Kuwaiti ambassador to Tehran told his country's daily newspaper *Sawt al-Kuwait* that Iran "must have a role in security arrangements" in the Gulf.[29] Correspondingly, the Kuwaiti government is much less easily influenced than it was before the war by propaganda attacks in the Arab media. For example, in response to those who criticized Kuwait for its tilt toward Iran and the West, the editor-in-chief of *Sawt al-Kuwait* said, "Every state has the right to select the party or parties which it deems most capable of helping it shoulder the burden of defense."[30] In other words, playing the role of spokesperson for the GCC, Kuwait has told Syria, and more particularly Egypt, to mind their own business. In September 1991, GCC members agreed on a formula for multilateral security cooperation with Iran, without negating the principles contained in the Damascus Declaration.[31] Later, Qatar signed an economic cooperation agreement with Iran that includes the building of a freshwater pipeline extending from Iran to Qatar. Kuwait is also considering a similar cooperation agreement.

While the Damascus Declaration raised concerns and misgivings in the Arabian Peninsula, it also constituted a new Arab coalition based on what the declaration describes as "cooperation, mutual respect, and noninterference in other countries' internal affairs."[32] The declaration kept the door open for other Arab states to join if they endorse those guiding principles. Egypt and Syria had high expectations from the new alliance, but the GCC states have repeatedly postponed ratifying it. At present it appears that, while Egypt and Syria would like to see the original terms of the agreement fulfilled, the GCC countries seem intent on watering down the signed document without scrapping it outright.[33]

Desert Storm also convinced the GCC of the critical importance of security pacts with the United States. The U.S. defense guarantee to Saudi Arabia proved valid in time of need as well as vital to the kingdom's survival. By contrast, Kuwait, which did not have a defense treaty with the United States, might have remained occupied had the U.S. government not considered the Iraqi invasion a genuine threat to the security of Saudi Arabia. Thus, Kuwait hurried to sign a 10-year security accord with the United States in September 1991, shortly after the war ended. The Kuwaiti foreign minister called it an "agreement on military cooperation, use of facilities, logistical support, pre-positioning of defense equipment, and legal status of U.S. forces in the State of Kuwait."[34] In justifying this pact, the minister alluded to a continuation of Iraqi "aggressive intentions." Such terrifying "intentions" led the Kuwaitis to sign two other defense accords with Britain and France in 1992 and to begin negotiating additional pacts with Russia and China.

Kuwait's bilateral security pacts with Western powers set the pace for all the remaining Gulf sheikhdoms. Bahrain signed a "defense cooperation accord" with the United States in late October 1991 without disclosing details.[35] Its rival, Qatar, signed a defense pact with the United States in June 1992.[36] Under these bilateral pacts, the United States will hold joint military exercises with the local Gulf forces, train these forces, have access to naval bases and other military facilities, and pre-position heavy equipment for use in emergency deployment missions.[37] The United States is planning similar agreements with Saudi Arabia and the United Arab Emirates.[38]

This drive to secure bilateral pacts with Western powers was due, in part, to the failure of the Gulf states to agree on a self-defense plan using their own armed forces. Although their subregional organization, the GCC, is the most coherent of the groupings in the Arab world, it is not entirely cohesive. The five small member states are not at ease with their far stronger partner, Saudi Arabia. In a culture such as that of the Arabs, the ethos of equality is strong and the stability of social and political relations among peers is threatened by the perception that relations are one-sided.[39] The extreme inequality that exists in the relationship between the small Gulf states and Saudi Arabia[40] has engendered neither stability nor trust in bilateral or multilateral relations. The border clash that took place between Qatari forces and some armed Saudis in October 1992 provides a recent example of instability.[41] Relations among the small GCC states are also characterized by disputes over territory and natural resources, a recent example of which is the dispute between Qatar and Bahrain over a number of territorial reefs and islands. These disputes are often compounded by personal rivalries between rulers.

RISE OF INTERSTATE DISPUTES

A number of border disputes remain unresolved in the Arab world,[42] but, until recently, few have proven explosive in nature or likely to escalate into violent conflicts with repercussions for the entire regional order. The dispute between Iraq and Kuwait that escalated into the invasion of Kuwait, however, has activated other longtime, latent disputes among Arab states. In addition to the Iraq-Kuwait conflict, two other disputes warrant special attention: the Saudi-Yemeni border issue and the Bahrain-Qatar dispute.

The Iraq-Kuwait Conflict

The Iraq-Kuwait border conflict did not end with Saddam's invasion of Kuwait, nor was it resolved by the liberation of Kuwait. The territorial dispute between the two states dates back to the 1930s, when Ghazi bin Faysal, then king of Iraq, proposed to the Kuwaiti ruler, and to the British, a union with Kuwait. King Ghazi's proposal was turned down. In 1961, Iraq's military ruler Abdul Karim Qassem pushed his troops into Kuwaiti territory following Britain's granting of independence to Kuwait, but his forces were repelled by the British. In 1973, Iraq moved its troops into northeast Kuwait, clashing with the Kuwaitis, but later withdrew its forces under pressure from Arab states.

While Iraq formally recognized the independence of Kuwait in 1963, it has only acceded to a loose definition of the boundaries specified in a 1932 exchange of correspondence with Britain.[43] Since then, it has consistently rejected these imposed borders, and a strong belief exists among Iraqi Arabs of various political persuasions that Kuwait is an integral part of Iraq.[44] In particular, Iraq has demanded the cession or lease of the islands of Warba and Bubiyan, which would considerably improve its access to the Gulf. It has also demanded a small plot of land to be used for the expansion of its port of Umm Qasr. These demands were repeatedly rejected by Kuwait and were among the factors that contributed to the Gulf crisis.

Further complicating the situation, the United Nations Iraq-Kuwait Boundary Demarcation Commission recommended in April 1992 moving the borderline some distance north of the prewar divide, thereby giving Kuwait several oil wells in Rumaila field and 3,000 feet of a former Iraqi naval base at the port of Umm Qasr.[45] While the Iraqi government rejected the commission's recommendation,[46]

Kuwaiti officials hailed its work as a "great achievement" that represents "the restoration of Kuwaiti rights."[47] The Security Council later approved the commission's demarcation line and told Baghdad it had to abide by its decision, warning it of "grave consequences" if it did not.[48]

Although the work of the UN commission may be technically impeccable and legally binding on Iraq, its disregard for Iraq's political sensitivities seems likely to make the new border a source of enduring contention. By imposing its decision, backed by the weight of Security Council enforcement mechanisms, rather than seeking a mutually acceptable arrangement, the United Nations provoked outrage among Iraqis, a sentiment that may well outlast Saddam.

The Saudi-Yemeni Dispute

The border dispute between Saudi Arabia and Yemen dates back to the 1930s but lay dormant until April 1992, when President Ali Abdullah Saleh of Yemen reopened it. In a press interview, he accused Saudi Arabia of laying claim to the oil-rich areas of Ma'reb, al-Jauf, and Hadramout in the former Democratic Yemen. The interview followed warnings by the Saudi foreign ministry to some of the oil companies working in Yemen that they were working in Saudi territory and that Riyadh would take "all measures to protect its rights against any illegal action."[49]

Despite Saleh's protest of the Saudi measures and his warning that "there are limits to Yemen's patience," he expressed readiness to negotiate with Saudi Arabia over border issues and what he termed "the historical and legal rights of Yemen,"[50] an implicit reference to the controversial 1934 Taef Treaty. Under the terms of this treaty, Saudi forces, which then occupied large tracts of Yemen, agreed to give up some of the captured tracts in return for leasing the provinces of Asir, Najran, and Jizan from then north Yemen. The treaty is renewable every 20 *hijri* (lunar) years and, according to Yemen, expired in September 1992.[51]

While the Yemeni foreign minister hinted at his country's desire to regain the ceded territory,[52] President Saleh appeared more conciliatory, calling for a discussion of the Taef Treaty along with other border and bilateral issues. Riyadh's reply, however, suggested a desire to base the negotiations on Yemen's prior approval of the 1934 treaty.[53] The Saudis also denied having any "territorial designs on the lands of others,"[54] while accusing Sanaa of obstructing a border demarcation agreement.

The simmering border dispute between Yemen and Saudi Arabia reflects the deterioration of their bilateral relations; it began during the Gulf crisis and was exacerbated by the expulsion of some 700,000 Yemenis working in Saudi Arabia. It also indicates a growing Saudi uneasiness regarding the nature of the newly reunified Yemen. Following the merger of the Yemen Arab Republic and the People's Democratic Republic of Yemen, the newly proclaimed Republic of Yemen has a population comparable in size to that of Saudi Arabia. Political participation is increasing, with national elections planned for April 1993. Freedom of the press and freedom of political expression have been expanded, and the country is taking impressive steps toward liberalization. By contrast, despite the growing influence of liberal, modernized groups, the Saudi government is still too heavily influenced by an aggressive fundamentalist element to be able to aim toward real liberalization.

In addition, oil production in Yemen is increasing, and studies suggest that more wells may be dug in the near future, particularly in areas claimed by Saudi Arabia. Such developments would improve social and economic conditions in Yemen and render the country economically independent of foreign aid, particularly from Saudi Arabia. The growth of political liberalization, or even democracy, combined with economic prosperity would make Yemen a strong competitor to Saudi Arabia in the Arabian peninsula.

An escalation of the Saudi-Yemeni dispute would jeopardize the stability and security of the Gulf region. Thus, the United States and other Western countries are unlikely to allow the dispute to grow too heated. Both official and unofficial attempts were made by a number of countries, notably the United States and the European Community, to mediate between the two countries. These efforts culminated in a bilateral meeting between Saudi and Yemeni diplomats in Geneva in July 1992, a prelude to rounds of meetings of experts from the two countries that began in Riyadh in September 1992. Although a final resolution may not easily be achieved, given the tense relations between the two countries, an interim settlement is not unlikely.

The Bahrain-Qatar Dispute

For decades Bahrain and Qatar have quarreled over ownership of a number of islands and reefs. All of these areas, including Fasht al-Deibal reef, the nearby Jarada island, and the Hawar islands just off the Qatar mainland, are presently controlled by Bahrain. Qatar rejected the British decision of the 1930s and 1940s to give these areas to Bahrain, noting that Fasht al-Deibal, for instance, is just off its large northern gas field. This dispute has created continuous tension between the two states, bringing them to blows in 1986, when Qatar landed helicopters on Fasht al-Deibal, arresting workers building a Bahraini coast guard post. In the wake of the Gulf War, Qatar and Bahrain exchanged harsh verbal accusations, and, in August 1991, a Qatari missile boat sailed into disputed territorial waters. Bahrain protested, reviving its old territorial claim to Zubara, the original home of its ruling family.[55] Saudi Arabia has continued to mediate between the two parties.

Since the end of the Gulf War, the Bahrain-Qatar dispute has impeded GCC cooperation by forcing postponement of several high-level meetings. Both Bahrain and Saudi Arabia desired a bilateral, or a Saudi-mediated resolution, yet, to their dismay, Qatar unilaterally took the dispute to the International Court of Justice in June 1991. In April 1992, Qatar also announced an extension of its territorial waters to 12 miles, with partial claims to an additional 12 miles. Several countries, including the United States and Britain, have urged the two parties to settle their dispute amicably, but such a settlement does not seem to be forthcoming. Bahrain has repeatedly proposed to Qatar the submission to the World Court of a joint application regarding their dispute, thereby indicating its acceptance of international arbitration,[56] but Qatar has persistently rejected these proposals.

During the recent escalation of the dispute—as during its confrontation with Saudi Arabia over border issues—Qatar moved to strengthen its relations with Iran in order to bolster its position vis-à-vis Bahrain. No doubt the Qatari government also hoped that close links with Tehran would reduce the intensity of long-standing Iranian claims on its offshore gas field, but Qatar's economic rapprochement with Iran[57] has caused anxiety among other GCC members; these members fear further Iranian involvement in GCC affairs, especially in the wake of the Iranian takeover of the half of the island of Abu Musa that was, until recently, under the control of the United Arab Emirates. Nevertheless, the security concerns of the Gulf sheikhdoms should have been somewhat alleviated by the conclusion of a defense agreement between the United States and Qatar in June 1992.

INTRODUCTION OF NON-ARAB POWERS TO THE ARAB ORDER

Desert Storm irrevocably widened the framework of the Arab regional order by enlarging the roles played by three regional actors—Israel,

Iran, and Turkey—and by increasing the influence of the United States, Britain, and France. The roles of these states are not equally important: Israel remains the major regional military power, while U.S. influence far exceeds that of Britain or France.

Israel has long been assured of a central role in regional politics primarily because of its military and organizational supremacy, unique strategic alliance with the United States, democratic political system, central location within the Middle East, and control of water resources. This central role has been further reinforced because the Gulf War neither neutralized nor weakened Israel's sources of power but considerably reduced the power of its Arab antagonists.

At the military level, Israel suffered negligible damage yet gained additional military and moral support from the United States and other states. By contrast, Iraq was devastated; Syria could not find a replacement for the former Soviet Union as a superpower protector and source of advanced weapons; and the PLO fell into disputes with former Arab allies and with Palestinian rebel groups, notably HAMAS. Although Israel's strategic importance to the United States appears to have declined following Desert Storm, the American government has stated that it remains "unshakably committed to Israel's security and to preserving Israel's qualitative edge over any likely combination of aggressors."[58]

In addition, Israel continues to be more industrialized than any of the Arab states, having considerably more efficient and productive organizations in a variety of economic and social activities, including business, education, and politics. Perhaps more important, to the extent that it represents Jewish residents, Israel is more democratic than any of the Arab regimes. Its record of human rights with regard to the Palestinians in the occupied territories, however, remains tarnished.

Another source of Israel's power is its control of water resources. At present, three major tributaries of the Jordan River and the Litani River in south Lebanon are under Israel's control. In the ongoing bilateral and multilateral Middle East negotiations, Israel could use this control to extract concessions from Jordan, Lebanon, and the Palestinians.

Iran's neutral stance in the Gulf crisis, combined with the declining influence of radicals within its political leadership, helped it to initiate better relations with the GCC countries immediately after the Gulf War. As mentioned earlier, some of these countries would like Iran to assume wider security responsibilities in the Gulf in order to counter a resurgence of Iraqi military power. But all of the

GCC members, including Saudi Arabia, have attempted to establish friendly relations with Iran, initially downplaying the recent dispute over Abu Musa island and putting behind them the memory of the Iran-Iraq War, in which the GCC states supported Iraq. However, Iran's insistence on retaining full control over Abu Musa and its threats to make other claims on Bahraini territory have now created tension in its relations with all GCC members except Qatar.

Iran is also reaching out to a number of other Arab countries, seeking to maintain old relationships and develop new alliances and friendly relations. It has widened its cooperation with the Sudan and Yemen and maintained good relations for a decade with Syria, Hizballah of Lebanon, and the Islamic opposition parties in Iraq, whose leaders and paramilitary forces are based on its territory. Iran has sought better relations with the Kurdish parties in Iraq, the Palestinian HAMAS, and other Islamic groups in the Arab world. Militarily, it is working to regain its power, following the long and devastating war with Iraq, by acquiring sophisticated weapons of all types, including weapons with mass destruction potential such as long-range missiles.

Turkey played an important role in Desert Storm. First, Turkey allowed the coalition forces access to its air bases and other military facilities. Since the end of the war, coalition aircraft have continued to use a Turkish air base for flights over northern Iraq designed to monitor the status of Saddam's army and to provide protection to the Kurds. Second, Turkey controls the pipeline that a UN resolution requires Iraq to use for all of its oil shipments, thereby rendering Iraq dependent on Turkey in this vital area. Third, and most important to the region—particularly to Iraq and Syria—Turkey controls the sources of the Euphrates and Tigris rivers. Both Syria and Iraq are highly dependent on water from these rivers and have been concerned about the reduced flow of Euphrates water to their countries resulting from the Southern Anatolia Development Program of Turkey.[59] This project aims at creating a huge lake, the water of which will be used for drinking, irrigation, and generation of electric power. To fill the lake, the flow of the Euphrates to Syria and Iraq has been reduced during several months since 1990. Competition over water resources with Turkey is a potentially explosive area of dispute that is currently being examined in multilateral Middle East negotiations.

Britain and France played important roles in Desert Storm as junior partners of the United States. Since then, they have managed to develop their relations with the Gulf states through bilateral security pacts (notably, with Kuwait), sales of weapons, and provision of military and civil training; in addition, French and British businesses have won many contracts in the Gulf region. Despite their enhanced roles in the region, however, Britain and France are unlikely to act independently of the United States.

Since August 1990, the United States has become more of a central player in Arab politics, both in the Gulf region and beyond. Through its leadership of the world coalition to liberate Kuwait and rid Iraq of its weapons of mass destruction, its postwar bilateral security pacts with the Gulf states, and its commitment to help resolve the Arab-Israeli conflict and other potentially explosive Middle Eastern disputes,[60] the United States has further integrated itself into the Arab regional order. No longer described in the state-controlled Arab media with pejorative epithets such as "imperialist," the United States has become the new Mecca to which many Arab parties turn.

U.S. companies continue to enjoy favored treatment in most Arab countries, particularly Egypt and the Gulf states. About half of the reconstruction contracts in Kuwait went to U.S. companies. Sales of U.S. weapons and military materiel to the Arab region have amounted to several billion dollars since the close of the war. In addition, the volume of trade transactions between the United States and the Gulf states and Egypt has increased since the end of the Gulf War.

CONCLUSION

With the decline of Iraq as a regional power, three states—Egypt, Saudi Arabia, and Syria—have assumed new roles in Arab affairs. Egypt's economic vulnerability, coupled with its much-reduced military power since the signing of the Camp David Accords, has made other Arab states less willing to accept its regional leadership and has left Egypt itself more dependent on Western economic aid. Saudi Arabia, which previously mediated inter-Arab conflicts, has now become a party to regional conflicts. Its former large clientele of aid recipients has been reduced to a small number of trusted allies. In its foreign policy, Saudi Arabia has become more aggressive, while growing more dependent on the United States for protection from external as well as internal threats. Syria is now the only Arab power that constitutes a military threat to Israel, a distinction that has engendered much concern within Syria about the likelihood of an Israeli preemptive strike against it. This preoccupation with its security has reduced the importance of Syria's wider role in regional politics, despite its continuing efforts to act as mediator between Iran and the Arab states.

The new Arab order is characterized by a deep fissure between the Gulf and non-Gulf states—that is, between the rich and the poor states—a rise in interstate border disputes, and an increased role played by non-Arab powers in the regional order. Desert Storm convinced the Arab Gulf states (the members of the GCC) of the critical importance of bilateral security pacts with the United States and the relatively minor significance of alliances with other Arab states and groups. Consequently, the GCC countries have become much more dependent on Western protection and less concerned about other Arabs. Besides the long-standing Kuwait-Iraq dispute, the border disputes between Qatar and Bahrain and between Saudi Arabia and Yemen could jeopardize the stability and security of the Gulf region.

The Gulf War has widened the framework of the Arab order by enlarging the roles played by three regional actors—Israel, Iran, and Turkey— and increasing the influence of Britain, France, and especially the United States. Through its leadership of Desert Storm, its bilateral security pacts with the Gulf states, and its active involvement in the Middle East peace process, the United States has further integrated itself into the Arab regional order.

six

The Prospects for Stability and Peace

𝕊𝕆 In many ways, the Gulf War has been a disaster for the Arab world. The elimination of Iraq as a viable military threat to the security of other Arab states has certainly been welcomed by most Arab governments, and the postwar revitalization of peace talks between Israel and its Arab neighbors and the Palestinians may produce positive moves toward peace, or at least accommodation. But the price the peoples and the governments of the Arab world have paid for these outcomes has been high. The changes wrought by the Gulf War—for example, in matters of economics, demographics, and interstate relations—have, for the most part, contributed to the instability of the region as a whole and of the states individually. The redirection or refashioning of existing conditions and attitudes brought about by the war—for instance, the growth of Islamism and the essential authoritarianism of most Arab regimes—have perpetuated, or even accentuated, potentially inflammatory forces. One cannot, of course, *blame* the Gulf War for these outcomes; the war was, after all, fought primarily to evict Iraq from Kuwait, and in that it succeeded. But the tendency displayed within some Western circles to ascribe to the war all sorts of beneficial effects must be corrected; in the Arab world at least, the war has created more problems than it has solved.

As the preceding chapters have detailed, the economic costs of the war have been enormous, even for members of the victorious coalition. The human costs have been substantial too. In addition to the scores of thousands of Iraqis killed during Desert Storm, hundreds of thousands of Kurds, Palestinians, Bedoons, and Yemenis have either become refugees or have been expelled from the countries in which they formerly resided, losing in the process both possessions and incomes and placing great strains on the countries to which they have relocated.

The Arab world is now perhaps a more dangerous place than it was before the war. The Iraqi threat is gone, at least for the time being, but in its aftermath the remaining vestiges of regional cooperation seem to have been stripped away, leaving a region more dependent on external assistance and more inclined toward internal belligerence. Peace is threatened not only by the resurrection of old disputes between states, but also by the potential for increased instability within states. Most Arab governments seem reluctant to offer their people more than token gestures of democracy, even though popular demands for real democratic reforms have grown significantly. The diminishing legitimacy of many regimes in the eyes of their people is further endangered by the continuing growth of Islamism as the ideology of popular dissent. The Gulf War has underscored, not undermined, the power of the Islamists.

This final chapter seeks to accomplish two purposes. First, it assesses the stability of each of the six countries featured in this study—Algeria, Egypt, Iraq, Kuwait, Jordan, and Saudi Arabia—and suggests which states are most susceptible to future strife unless their governments take appropriate corrective actions. Second, it addresses the impact of the Gulf War on the future of the Arab-Israeli peace process. By tipping the military balance in the Middle East in favor of Israel and by dispelling certain myths among Arabs about their eventual victory over Israel, the Gulf War has increased Arab preparedness to negotiate with the old enemy. However, as the country-by-country survey indicates, one must avoid generalizing about Arab attitudes and instead examine each state's options and ambitions separately.

STABILITY OF ARAB REGIMES

Although none of the Arab regimes, including those of Iraq and Kuwait, was toppled as a result of the war, the legitimacy of most has been increasingly questioned by their citizens. Popular demands for real, as opposed to cosmetic, reform in various areas—political, social, and economic—are on the rise. Islamist-dominated political oppositions have gained support, particularly in the non-Gulf states, and some small groups are turning more violent and uncompromising. The combination of high population growth, authoritarian or oligarchic leadership, and stagnant, militarized economies has contributed to political instability in a number of countries. This instability is exacerbated by the continued conflict over the Palestine question and other interstate disputes. Each of the destabilizing factors, however, weighs differently in different countries, and the set of relevant factors is not the same in every Arab state. Thus, it is useful to examine each of the selected cases separately.

Algeria

In the years preceding the Gulf War, the Algerian government was unstable, plagued by abysmal economic conditions and state mismanagement and corruption. Conditions did not improve during the short term of office of the late Boudiaf, who made more foes than friends. He crushed the Islamist FIS, refusing any subsequent meetings with its leaders. He also antagonized the former ruling party, the FLN, and the army generals who brought him to power by vowing to eradicate state corruption and attempting to create a power base for himself through the "patriotic forum" while failing to halt the country's economic collapse. By March 1992, food prices had tripled,[1] and on the eve of his assassination, the external economic aid pledged by the European Community had not arrived.

The death of Boudiaf and the aftereffects of the Gulf War have made Algeria's problems even more difficult to resolve. The war imposed major economic hardships on all of the Gulf states, thereby reducing the amount of assistance they are able to extend. In addition, since January 1992 the legitimacy of the High Committee of State (HCS), which was imposed by the military, has been contested, leading to continuous social unrest. Violence has escalated, manifested by renewed armed assaults against policemen, battles between armed Islamists and police, and recurrent protest demonstrations that clash with police.[2] So far, Ali Kafi, the new HCS president, has shown no signs of conciliation toward the FIS. These conditions have led to a new hesitation on the part of international donors to proceed with their pledged contributions to the country's economic revival.

The establishment of regime legitimacy in Algeria is necessary for political stability. Although a government that lacks widespread popular support can win approval if it succeeds in bringing prosperity, such an outcome is unlikely in Algeria. So far, the present leadership has not initiated economic reforms, and the state bureaucracy suffers from incompetence at a time of global economic slowdown. The army may have succeeded in suppressing the FIS, but the rise of political Islam cannot be stemmed through such measures. Brutal repression may, in fact, strengthen it, leading to the birth of new movements better suited to pursuing their goals by using violence.

Egypt

Egypt's efforts to improve its economy by embarking on an economic liberalization program and making peace with Israel have not yielded prosperity. Economic reform policies have been resisted by corrupt bureaucrats whose vested interests are threatened, and, despite large-scale international assistance, Egypt's external debt remains substantial—about $26 billion—while the unemployment rate stands at 20 percent.[3]

Egypt's persistent high population growth is, by itself, a recipe for instability in a poor, authoritarian state.[4] The ever-increasing numbers of youths from all walks of life who are looking for jobs in a slow-growing economy jeopardize the cohesion of the social fabric and the confidence between the people and their rulers. The demographic-economic problem is further complicated by the battle raging between secularists and Islamic fundamentalists for the hearts and minds of the Egyptian people. Even though the economic and demographic impact of the Gulf War on Egypt has not been severe enough to pose a real threat to the regime's stability,[5] war-related demographic and economic troubles, combined with other social and political factors, could produce an explosive situation.

There are two major sociopolitical threats to stability: the regime's ambivalence toward Islamic fundamentalism and its apparent lack of a commitment to democratization.[6] Mubarak's administration is essentially secular and declares all political parties based on religion illegal; at the same time, however, it has appealed to Islamic fundamentalists by means of administrative measures, such as blocking the construction of new Christian churches, providing high visibility to fundamentalist clerics, and claiming that its policies and laws are commensurate with the *shari'a*.

The majority of the Egyptian people are Muslims, and an opinion poll in *al-Ahram* recently showed that most of them would like to apply the *shari'a*. Given this popular sentiment, the Egyptian government might advance the cause of political stability by demonstrating its true commitment to democratic principles[7] and legitimizing Islamic parties. After all, Islam does not lend itself to only one—the fundamentalist—interpretation;[8] Islamic liberals are no less Islamic than Islamic fundamentalists. Any party that adheres to a minimum set of democratic principles could be allowed to operate openly and not forced to go underground or to resort to violence to pursue its goals. The benefits of such a policy can be seen in Jordan, which successfully integrated political pluralism into a hereditary monarchy in 1991 when various parties, including the Islamic Brotherhood, signed the National Charter.

So far, the Egyptian regime has been among the more stable in the Middle East, partly because of the long tradition of tolerance in Egypt. But such stability is under threat. Signs of dissent and challenge to the government have become recurrent, and violence is increasingly used by new and revived opposition groups that are denied freedom of expression and organization. Coptic Christians are more worried than ever about their safety and future, and their organizations in Western countries are calling on the West for protection.[9] If the regime is to preserve the nation's stability, it needs to stem the rising tide of dissatisfaction and violence. So far, repression does not seem to have been successful in this regard, suggesting that a bold step toward democratization might be the only effective means of quelling widespread dissent. Unfortunately, however, few signs indicate that the government is prepared to take such a step. Instability, therefore, seems likely to worsen.

Iraq

The massive bombings conducted by U.S.-led coalition forces inflicted heavy economic, political, social, and human losses on Iraq. The postwar continuation of economic sanctions against Iraq and the halting of the smuggling of goods through Jordan, coupled with U.S. and Arab Gulf support for various opposition groups, have weakened the regime. In the United States and elsewhere, many policy analysts have concluded that the Iraqi regime has withered to such an extent that it will crumble under any additional pressure. Such assessments, however, have been based largely on Western intelligence information that so far has proved to be only occasionally accurate.[10]

This author's analysis leads to a different conclusion. As a number of scholars have observed, the internal cohesion of a group may be enhanced by its entering into conflict with another group.[11] External threats to a social system often result in internal forces putting aside their differences and joining together to confront the common enemy. This has apparently taken place among a large segment of the Sunni Arabs of Iraq, who constitute the core of the regime's popular power base. Although this development is hard to prove conclusively and empirically, it does seem to tally with the following observations.

First, unlike Westerners, Arabs in general, and Muslims in particular, do not quickly discredit a longtime leader, even when he fails drastically. Notable examples of this phenomenon are Nasser and Yasir Arafat, both of whom made serious political blunders while strong external forces were trying to dislodge them. Yet, there is no doubt that Nasser remained popular until his death, and Arafat has so far maintained wide support among the Palestinian people. To the dismay of his numerous enemies, Saddam Hussein continues to be a hero in the eyes of millions of Arabs—Jordanians, Palestinians, Algerians, Tunisians, Yemenis, and Sudanese. During the war, the Algerians, for instance, used to call him *fahl*, a term that connotes outstanding virility and strength, for confronting the superpower and for fulfilling his promise to attack Israel if he were attacked by the coalition first.[12] American visitors to these countries in the wake of the war felt that popular support for Iraq and Saddam was still strong.

Second, during the postwar uprisings, many Shiite and Kurdish rebels committed atrocities against Sunni Arabs. The Shiites also revealed their adherence to Iranian-style politics through their slogans and demands. The Sunni Arabs were thus warned of the danger if Saddam were overthrown, a possibility that was skillfully exploited by the government to drive a wedge between the Sunni Arabs, on the one hand, and the Shiite Arabs and the Sunni Kurds, on the other. The likelihood of ethnic killings in the event of a takeover by a weak regime (as occurred in the case of Lebanon) may have accentuated people's fears. To the Sunni Arabs, no better alternative is available, partly because Saddam has kept purging his subordinates and eliminating potential rivals, and partly because a military coup not only would be bloody, but also would bring another dictator to power.

Third, neither the continuation of sanctions against Iraq nor the limited Western air strikes launched in January 1993 have led to rebellion against Saddam. Instead, he has managed to nurture feelings of resentment and hostility toward the United States and the Arab Gulf states. Even many Arabs outside Iraq are voicing their humanitarian concerns, calling for a halt to the sanctions, which are causing far more human suffering than is the regime. Given the depth of anti-American feeling prevailing among the Iraqis caused by U.S. insistence on maintaining sanctions until Saddam falls, it is not likely that the people will rise up to oust Saddam in favor of another dictator.

Fourth, Saddam's dependence on a small core of loyalist kin who are in key positions in the army, security bodies, and the Ba'ath party, and his elaborate security network have provided him with exceptional power as well as an extraordinarily cohesive ruling group. Stories of postwar coups have been closer to rumor than fact, with no hard evidence yet presented. The high level of internal cohesion within an extremely authoritarian regime under external threat diminishes the likelihood of coups despite the formidable combination of antagonistic foreign powers. Even if such a coup succeeded, it would bring to power another Sunni despot, most likely from Saddam's family, village, or entourage.

Fifth, the opposition parties are too numerous and divided to pose a real threat to the regime. Despite all the external support and assistance extended to help them agree on a political formula for a post-Saddam Iraq, nothing significant has so far materialized. Although the number of opposition parties is ever increasing, they are still ineffective in changing the status quo. More important, while the Shiite and Sunni insurgents are leading their crusade against Saddam from neighboring and Western countries, the extent of their domestic support is uncertain. Only the Kurds were organized and determined enough to challenge the regime and establish an autonomous region.

Does this mean that the regime is stable and invincible? As far as the Sunni Arabs are concerned, the regime has proved to be resilient and may remain in place, with or without Saddam, for many more years. As long as the Sunni Arabs perceive that the territorial integrity of Iraq is in danger and the threat of Iranian control of the state through their local surrogates is looming, their solidarity with the regime is likely to continue unabated. Only when the external threats are far removed, as was the case for Egypt after Camp David, are popular demands for political reform and personal freedoms likely to prevail.

The relationship of the regime, and the Sunni Arabs generally, with the Shiite majority has turned sour and tense as a result of the uprising in the south, a situation that may lead to occasional confrontations. However, there are no indications that such confrontations, or the enforcement of a southern no-fly zone, can destabilize the government, which continues to use a carrot-and-stick approach toward the Shiites. Any new Shiite uprising, even if supported by

Iran and other powers, is unlikely to topple the regime because of the wide disparity in military power between the two. It may succeed, however, in initiating a civil war between the Shiites in the south and the Sunnis led by Saddam or his successors. The most such a war could achieve is the creation of an autonomous region or independent Shiite state in the south, which would be as appalling to the Saudis, whose Shiites live in areas bordering the south of Iraq, as it would be to the Iraqi regime.

The establishment of a civil administration for the Kurdish region has alarmed not only the Iraqi and other Arab regimes, but also neighboring states such as Turkey, which has 12 million Kurdish inhabitants. Assertions by Kurdish leaders that they do not intend to create a separate state are not reassuring. A de facto state can still emerge if the present protected status of Kurdistan continues indefinitely. In the light of the likelihood of UN approval for the lifting of economic sanctions against Kurdistan, which is legally still part of Iraq, this is even more conceivable. As time goes by, new realities created on the ground will be hard to change. And regardless of the wishes and demands of the United States and neighboring countries, "Free Kurdistan" could become the prototype for an independent Kurdish state.

If such a state is created, or seems likely to be created, both Iraq and Turkey will oppose it violently, thereby adding another chapter to the familiar story of displacement in the area. The Iraqi regime still shows no signs of forgiving the Kurds for rejecting its autonomy proposal and seeking Western protection. On the contrary, Saddam's son, editor of the daily *Babel*, has used the press repeatedly to threaten Kurdish leaders with punishment, an action that may have to await withdrawal of the Western forces from Turkey.

Thus it seems that the Iraqi regime is still in control of its Arab population and is preparing to regain control of the Kurdish region as soon as the regional and international situation permits. Nevertheless, the losses incurred as a result of the war and postwar uprisings have considerably diminished Iraq's military might, thereby reducing its potential threat to its neighbors. If economic sanctions were lifted, the regime's internal political problems might well be aggravated by the emergence of popular demands for reform, while the people's agonies would be somewhat relieved.

Kuwait

With the departure of most of the Palestinians formerly resident there, Kuwait has relieved itself of its longtime commitment to the

Palestine cause. Indeed, the regime is now antagonistic toward the Palestinians and took the extreme measure of declaring the entire Palestinian population undesirable "traitors." Rather than endorsing the Damascus Declaration that calls for an Egyptian and Syrian role in Gulf security, Kuwait opted for bilateral security pacts with the United States, Britain, and France and called for an Iranian role in Gulf security. Thus, in addition to its conflict with Iraq, which the new UN-imposed border demarcation will help sustain, and its hostility toward the Palestinians, the Yemenis, and the Sudanese, the emirate's relations with Egypt and Syria have deteriorated following the short-term rapprochement brought about by the Gulf crisis. This is a drastic turnaround from the cordial relations that it enjoyed with almost all Arab states and peoples in the prewar period.

Kuwait's strong tilt toward American protection and shunning of Arab support will almost certainly bode ill for the emirate in future disputes with its neighbors. U.S. forces can certainly maintain the Sabahs in power and keep their state resistant to incursions from its neighbors; however, the American presence could also discredit the Kuwaiti rulers as U.S. puppets and isolate them from their Arab environment.

On the domestic front, the royal family is being increasingly challenged by an emerging, modernized middle class that is forcefully demanding genuine political reform. The National Assembly elections that were held in October 1992 were widely regarded as free and fair. Most (72 percent) of the 50 elected members belonged to one or other of the opposition parties, half of whom were affiliated with Islamist groups. Liberals and reformists comprised the other half of the assembly's opposition.[13] The results of the elections have enhanced the credibility of the Kuwaiti government, but they have also increased the pressure on it to be more accountable to the electorate. The possibility of a peaceful transition to less authoritarian rule is real; however, disputes over the course of the political transformation are certain to continue and may strain the royal family's tolerance of further political reform.

Jordan

Jordan has shown resilience in the face of unprecedented destabilizing forces, both internal and external. The influx of some 300,000 Palestinians from the Gulf at a time when the economy was declining and unemployment was in double digits posed real dangers to the political stability of the kingdom. Jordan was also confronted with conflicting pressures from Iraq and the coalition to join their forces during the Gulf crisis. Although Jordan's neutral stance and its desire for an Arab-sponsored resolution to the conflict seem to have been accepted by Iraq, the Arab Gulf states considered that position traitorous and supportive of Saddam.

Two and a half years after the beginning of the Gulf crisis, Jordan's economy remains in dire straits, a situation that poses a threat to the stability of a regime that has so far depended heavily on foreign aid and remittances from emigrants abroad.[14] Both sources of support have been greatly reduced. Arab aid was cut as a punishment for the regime taking what was perceived to be a pro-Iraq stand in the Gulf War. Remittances diminished substantially as a result of the massive out-migration of Jordanians and Palestinians, mainly from Kuwait and Iraq. There are two other potential sources of instability: the revival of the Palestine issue brought about by the creation of a Palestinian majority in Jordan, and the resurgence of political Islam as an ideology of opposition that justifies revolt against non-Islamic behavior and calls for the forceful liberation of Palestine from Israeli rule.

The destabilizing effect of the Palestinian issue is counterbalanced by Jordan's active involvement in the Middle East peace process with Israel. Progress on this front could reinforce domestic stability, whereas a stalemate could have an adverse effect. The rise of Islamic fundamentalism has been offset by the legalization of various political parties, most of which differ with the Islamists over major political and social issues. By allowing a variety of political currents and groups some freedom of expression and organization under the National Charter, the regime has so far managed to contain political dissent and prevent a damaging showdown with the opposition, particularly the Islamists. Nevertheless, historical experience indicates that wider political participation and freedom of expression may alter the nature of the state and its institutions. Although this is likely to be destabilizing in the short run, it ultimately may be a source of long-term stability.

Under such circumstances, and in view of the continued popularity of Saddam Hussein in Jordan and the deep sympathy that the Jordanian people have expressed for the suffering Iraqis, government adoption of an openly anti-Iraq policy would be tantamount to political and economic suicide, particularly in the atmosphere of increased political liberalization. While maintaining its commitment to a strict observance of UN sanctions against Iraq, the regime cannot afford to come out too strongly against individuals and companies that are defying the embargo. There is a limit to the tolerance of Jordanians for a strict, extended enforcement of the sanctions, as their economy is highly dependent on Iraq. This situation would be unlikely to change in the event of King Hussein's sudden death or resignation due to illness. An increase in U.S. pressure on Jordan to maintain the embargo indefinitely could jeopardize the stability of the regime, which would, in turn, jeopardize the Middle East peace process.

Saudi Arabia

With its overwhelmingly Sunni Arab population and its adherence to a strict interpretation of the *shari'a* as law, Saudi Arabia is one of the more stable states in the region and is certainly the most stable of the six countries under study. After many years of political and social stagnation during the 1930s and 1940s, the discovery of oil eventually led to increasing interdependence between the kingdom and the West, particularly the United States, thus exposing the previously secretive desert state to new and destabilizing forces. During Desert Storm, non-Muslim forces were summoned to protect the kingdom, an action that revealed Saudi Arabia's vulnerability and deep-rooted alliance with the West. This event was deeply disturbing to many conservative Saudis, who continue to view their state as the epitome of righteous Wahhabi Islam. Now that the Iraqi military threat has receded, the kingdom's adherence to puritan Islam has been questioned by new groups that are more fundamentalist than the regime itself.

At the same time, an increasing number of Saudis educated in the West and influenced by some of its liberal ideals are demanding a greater voice in the management of state affairs. This demand has been matched by a similar one from the conservative clerics. Both groups helped to speed up the preparation of the 1992 statutes of government that called for the creation of an appointed advisory council in which both forces will be represented. Despite the council's limited authority, its creation signifies a positive change in a long-stagnant system. Although he is not bound by them, the king cannot ignore the council's recommendations for new legislation or modifications of existing practices. He will have to find a way to satisfy, at least in part, both the liberal and the conservative demands, or risk regime instability.

Although the divergent forces of conservatism and modernity may destabilize the kingdom in the future, the enormous wealth of the state and its slow pace of change in social norms and mores has so far helped the royal family win the good graces of most domestic critics. Using a carrot-and-stick approach, the royal family has managed to reduce the traditional tensions between the residents of the regions of Hijaz and Najd (to which the Saudi rulers belong) and to marginalize the threat of potentially rebellious groups—notably, the Shiites and the Zaydis. As the oil wealth of Saudi Arabia is enormous and is not expected to be depleted soon, and as the regime is not likely to embrace democratization in the foreseeable future, the Saudi dynasty, with U.S. military support, could stay in power indefinitely.

POSTWAR CHANGES AND MIDDLE EAST PEACE

In destroying the military might of Iraq, the United States not only tipped the balance of military power in the Middle East heavily in Israel's favor, but also shattered some myths that had lingered among Arabs for decades. Egypt had already rid itself of these myths when it decided to normalize relations with Israel. The Egyptian government took this dramatic step for pragmatic reasons: It concluded that it was impossible to regain by force all the territory lost to Israel in previous wars; it recognized the depth of the U.S. commitment to Israel's security; it saw that pan-Arabism was in sharp decline; and it believed that the enormous resources that militarization would consume could be better spent improving the general welfare of the population.

Other Arab states were less willing to dispense with the myth that they could attain strategic military parity with Israel as a prelude to regaining their lost land and establishing a Palestinian state in place of Israel. Gradually, however, Arab governments, and an increasing number of people, have become aware of one important fact with regard to the Jewish state: The qualitative military edge Israel has over any likely combination of Arab forces is based on a permanent U.S. commitment to Israel's security.[15] The United States would not, under any circumstances, compromise Israel's security within safe borders.

All attempts to defeat Israel militarily on the battlefield and by incursions of Palestinian and other paramilitary commando forces have so far failed. Even Egypt's initial, limited victory in the 1973 war did not result in the liberation of the Sinai, which took several more years of negotiations, with active American involvement. Thus, Arab fighters have been forced to conclude that they must learn to accept and accommodate the Jewish state. Today, all members of the Arab League, including the PLO, openly endorse UN Resolutions 242 and 338, which call for the recognition of the state of Israel and its right to exist within safe borders in return for its withdrawal from occupied territories.

Another myth was the notion that pan-Arab solidarity would surface when one or more Arab parties engaged in a conflict with non-Arabs. Recurrent evidence showed the irrelevance of pan-Arabism years before the Gulf crisis, but the crisis provided another stark confirmation.[16] The failure of the Arabs to resolve the Iraq-Kuwait conflict peacefully, and the transparent absence of pan-Arab solidarity when the Iraqi army was attacked and defeated by the Western coalition troops in Desert Storm, proved once and for all the fictitious quality of pan-Arabism. Given this experience, it is unlikely that the Arabs will be able to take unified action toward a peaceful resolution of issues like the Arab-Israeli conflict.

Desert Storm neutralized Iraq's ability to sabotage a prospective peace process through an Arab third party. Jordan and the PLO were weakened and censured by their victorious Arab brothers for showing sympathy toward Iraq during the Gulf crisis. Consequently, both were willing to participate in the peace process, hoping to reduce their war-related losses and possibly gain some of their perceived rights. They took this step even without pressure from moderate Arab states. The U.S. administration seized the opportunity and initiated a two-track peace process, a bilateral and a multilateral negotiations track. The process had been faltering until the 1992 Labor party victory in Israel increased the possibility of its reinvigoration.

Given the destabilizing social, political, and economic forces at play in their countries and across the region,[17] by January 1993 the status quo was, for the negotiating Arabs, more "dangerous than a potential negotiated compromise."[18] Arabs generally agree that two main goals must be achieved through negotiations: withdrawal of Israeli forces from occupied territories and assertion of the Palestinians' right of self-determination. Consequently, they were eager to resume talks with Israel with the objective of restoring their occupied land, or at least part of it, prior to reaching a peace accord.

Yet, each of the Arab parties to the negotiations has its own, often distinct interests and agenda, which prevent the formation of a united front. This situation is to be expected, given the collapse of pan-Arab ideology and regional solidarity and the prevalence of a host of interstate disputes.[19]

As discussed in previous chapters, the postwar social, political, and economic changes have been different for each Arab country. The remainder of this chapter, in which the relationship between these changes and the nature of involvement in the peace process is analyzed, thus focuses on each country separately. Of the six countries or peoples examined below, three have played active roles in the peace talks: Egypt and Saudi Arabia as observers and facilitators and Jordan as a participant. Attention is also given to the roles played by the Palestinians, Syria, and Lebanon.

Egypt

Egypt has a vital interest in facilitating the Arab-Israeli peace talks as well as in playing an active role in them. It is a leading power in the Arab world, is at the helm of the Arab League, and is the only Arab state that has signed a peace accord with Israel. By agreeing in the Camp David Accords to the proposal for Palestinian autonomy, it assumed some responsibility for finding a peaceful solution to the Palestinian problem. Egypt sees the peace process as one way to rebuild its regional stature and prove its importance. Another reason for Egypt's interest in furthering Middle East peace is its inability to proceed with normalization of relations with Israel while the latter continues to be in a state of war with all the other "ring" states and the PLO. New peace agreements with other Arab countries, particularly Jordan and the Palestinians, are necessary in order for Egypt to move from the state of unstable peace—what the Israeli scholar Shimon Shamir terms "cold peace"—to a stable, warm peace. In the absence of such agreements, the regime's stability and legitimacy will become tremendously strained. In addition, Egypt and Syria justified their participation in Desert Storm on the assumption that the United States would initiate new efforts to resolve the Arab-Israeli conflict following the liberation of Kuwait.

Thus, the Egyptian government was anxious to engage in various aspects of the negotiations. Egypt's credentials led the United States, as well as some of the parties to the dispute, to invite it to play the role of facilitator, bridging misperceptions, mistrust, and recurrent lapses in communication between the Arabs and the Israelis. While the United States remains the only credible third party in the peace process, Egypt has played a significant auxiliary role, giving the United States necessary support, advice, and Arab cover. Given its experience in narrowing the differences between the disputants, Egypt's role is expected to be maintained in future peace talks and

possibly upgraded to that of a third party in partnership with the
United States.

Saudi Arabia

After many years of shying away from dealing with Israel and world
Jewry, postwar Saudi Arabia has adopted a position regarding the
Middle East peace process that is close to the positions of Egypt and
the United States. In November 1991, shortly after the Madrid conference, Prince Bandar bin Sultan, Saudi ambassador to the United
States, held his first public meeting with about 60 leading members
of the American Jewish community. As a representative of his government, the prince not only affirmed Saudi Arabian adherence to
UN Resolution 242, but also declared that "Israel is an integral part
of the region" and that the kingdom was committed to promoting
peace. Perhaps more important was his offer to assist in ending the
Arab economic boycott of Israel, as well as the *intifada*, in return
for a freeze on settlement building.[20]

Two weeks later, the leading Saudi daily, *Asharq al-Awsat*, interviewed a number of prominent American Jews who favor peace in
the Middle East. In December 1991 Saudi Arabia, a leading member
of the Islamic Conference Organization (ICO), endorsed a significant change in ICO's political agenda. For the first time in 10 years,
the ICO summit in Dakar dropped its 1981 call for a *jihad* against
Israel from its concluding resolutions, despite Arafat's vehement
opposition.[21] This was another clear sign of Saudi support for the
peace process.

Even before these events, the Saudi role in Madrid signaled an
important shift in foreign policy toward a more assertive and candid
expression of the kingdom's real interests and positions. Previously,
such expressions were vague or tacit and accompanied by cautious
or timid political gestures. The Gulf War changed this approach by
forcing Saudi Arabia to separate its friends from its enemies in the
Arab world. Desert Storm and its aftermath exposed Saudi vulnerability and need for U.S. protection, which in turn impelled the
Saudis to offer an open endorsement of U.S. peace efforts. Denials
on the part of the United States notwithstanding, Desert Storm also
revealed the existence of a link between the Arab-Israeli conflict
and other regional conflicts, at least in the minds of the Arabs.

Thus, it is in the best interests of the Saudis to help resolve this
conflict before Saddam, his successor, or another Arab despot has
an opportunity to exploit it to stir Arab revolts against the status

quo. Saddam's linkage of the Gulf conflict with the Palestinian issue showed that the security of the Gulf states and their oil resources remains at risk until the Arab-Israeli dispute is settled. The recent efforts on the part of the Saudis to ensure the success of the Arab-Israeli talks, particularly the multilateral negotiations boycotted by the Syrians and the Lebanese, reflect Saudi Arabia's serious, strategic commitment to, and continuous, active role in, the peace process. The kingdom's assertive participation, based on its role as the foremost regional financial power capable of providing economic incentives and disincentives to other participants, is unlikely to decline in the near future, as the peace process is vital to Saudi national security and prosperity.

Jordan

Apart from Egypt, Jordan is the first Arab state to try to resolve some aspects of its dispute with Israel through secret negotiations and meetings between the two nations' representatives and rulers. As Israeli writers have discovered,[22] it has also been a guarantor against "terrorist" incursions into Israel. Now that the Jordanian economy is in crisis and the increased Palestinian presence has tipped the demographic balance in favor of those who have a claim on the occupied territory, the Jordanian monarchy is facing the risk of losing power to the Palestinians, especially their Islamist groups. Although none of these groups has yet declared such an objective, the regime must be ever vigilant.

It is very important for the kingdom to defuse this potential danger to its existence by finding a peaceful settlement to the Palestinian problem—a settlement that, at the same time, does not create new security worries. It is not in Jordan's interests to have on its borders an independent Palestinian state ruled by extremists. For both political and economic reasons, Jordan is also concerned with the status of the refugees in its territory and has thus participated energetically in the multilateral sessions. In future peace talks, assuming no changes in the domestic political balance of power, Jordan is expected to remain engaged in sincere and serious discussions with Israel to resolve their dispute and sign a peace agreement.

The Palestinians

Next to Iraq itself, the Palestinians suffered the greatest political and economic losses as a result of the Gulf crisis. Their mass exodus from Kuwait and their ongoing feuds with Kuwait, Saudi Arabia, and other Gulf states have deprived them of considerable financial and political support. Although the Palestinians have long asserted their right of return to their previous homes in Israel in accordance with UN Resolution 194 of 1948, and have sought either repatriation or compensation of refugees in accordance with that resolution,[23] armed struggle against Israel has not brought them any military victory, nor has the *intifada* forced the Israelis out of the occupied territories. Consequently, along with Jordan, the PLO and a majority of Palestinians now appear ready to make peace with Israel in return for a recognition of their right of self-determination and the withdrawal of Israeli forces from the West Bank and Gaza. So far, Israel has agreed to offer only limited autonomy with the details to be negotiated.

However, the rise of Islamism within Palestinian ranks, especially following the PLO exodus from Lebanon in 1982, has complicated the situation. The strong appeal that political Islam holds for Palestinians has created a deep fissure between Islamic groups—notably, between HAMAS and the Palestinians' widely acknowledged representative, the PLO. Since both are active participants in the *intifada*, which after faltering for some time has in early 1993 been rekindled, the direction of the future Palestinian relations with Israel remains subject to changes in the balance of power between the PLO and the Islamists. Confronted with increasing hardship and failing political agendas, the Palestinians are unable to take a unified position toward the peace process. When Israel signaled its desire to make some concessions, the internal division among the Palestinians grew wider, precipitating internecine strife, such as was manifested in Gaza in the summer of 1992.

Although Palestinian political decision making is in the hands of the Fateh-dominated PLO, it is strongly influenced by a host of internal and external forces. There are two principal groups of internal forces: HAMAS and Palestinian independent leaders in the West Bank and Gaza (some with known personal links to Arafat, although they are not registered members of the PLO). The independent leaders advocate a negotiated peace settlement with Israel, whereas HAMAS and other militant Islamist groups reject any deals with Israel, calling instead for the armed liberation of Palestine and destruction of the state of Israel.

Regional forces include Israel, Syria, Jordan, Egypt, and Saudi Arabia, as well as the United States. All of these forces favor the peace talks, however Syria is firmly opposed to any bilateral agreements between an Arab party and Israel that have not been approved by all other Arab parties.[24] It is committed to a comprehensive settlement as an end product of bilateral negotiations. Jordan is also fearful of being excluded from an agreement between Israel and the Palestinians, but its position is less difficult to accommodate than that of Syria; thus Palestinian and Jordanian representatives have already begun to discuss the future of their relations.

In striving to foster Palestinian unity, the PLO's political decision-making process must take the conflicting views of different groups—both within and outside the organization—into consideration. The PLO cannot finalize a deal with Israel, either directly or through non-PLO representatives, unless the proposed settlement is significantly better than the current status quo under Israeli occupation. Otherwise, the Palestinian negotiators may walk out of the talks or opt for what a Bir Zeit professor called a "cul-de-sac option,"[25] meaning that the peace talks would follow the path former Israeli Prime Minister Yitzhak Shamir planned and thus head nowhere. It would be politically risky for the PLO and Palestinian moderates in the occupied territories to accept the Camp David proposal as it is presently constituted regarding the Palestinians (the proposal grants the Palestinians the right to their own civil administration in the occupied territories, but falls short of genuine self-government). An innovative formula that also takes Israeli security into account must be found in order to make a compromise worth the risk for the Palestinians.[26]

Syria

The Syrian population and economy were not adversely affected by the Gulf War. On the contrary, its economy has undergone rapid expansion, marked by rising private-sector activity.[27] Although it was largely symbolic, Syrian participation in Desert Storm has brought it closer to Egypt and the Gulf states and improved its relations with the United States. However, the loss of Soviet backing, combined with the lack of full-fledged U.S. support, has restricted its ability to influence regional politics. By agreeing to participate in bilateral talks, Syria made a significant concession on the procedure for conducting the peace process; at the same time, however, it has maintained its insistence on a comprehensive approach. Meanwhile, repeated U.S. assertions that the Golan Heights are occupied Arab territory have encouraged continued Syrian participation.

Of all of the remaining bilateral disputes between Israel and the Arabs, the dispute between Israel and Syria is the thorniest. Syria, a staunch advocate of pan-Arabism and defiant of Israel's supremacy, is unwilling to surrender its sovereignty over the Golan Heights. Such a move would undermine much of the legitimacy of Hafez al-Assad's regime. The domestic political considerations that have rendered successive Israeli governments, both Likud and Labor, unable to negotiate a final settlement with Syria in tandem with an interim agreement with the Palestinians are an additional complication. Since the Palestinians in the occupied territory pose an immediate and constant threat to Israel's security and welfare, and since the Camp David Accords contained an autonomy proposal for them, it was both feasible and desirable for Israel to negotiate a separate settlement with them. By contrast, Syria has not posed a real, direct threat to Israel's security for over a decade and has carefully kept its borders with Israel inaccessible to Arab militants.

With Yitzhak Rabin in power in Israel, Syria is wary of a deal likely to be made between Israel and either Jordan or the Palestinians that would weaken Syria's negotiating power and delay resolution of the Golan issue. To preempt such a development, Syria warned the PLO not to make a separate agreement with Israel and allowed the Palestinian opposition groups to issue a statement from Damascus rejecting the PLO policy of peace with Israel and expressing their commitment to foil Rabin's peace plan. Syria also invited the Arab participants in the negotiations to attend the first of several coordination meetings in Damascus, in which the participants reaffirmed their long-standing pledge to work toward a comprehensive settlement with Israel. In subsequent coordination meetings, Syria has continued to play a leading role.

Although Syria would like to end its state of war with Israel, the conditions imposed by the Israeli government remain unacceptable. One way to break the deadlocked bilateral talks could be to find an interim agreement that might be signed simultaneously with an agreement between Israel and the Palestinians.[28] Otherwise, Syria's frustration with the process seems sure to grow and may encourage it to turn a blind eye to actions to sabotage bilateral accords, especially through the activities of extremist groups and the Palestinian opposition—notably, HAMAS. Although a large-scale war may be unlikely to occur in the short run and would be bound to fail in the long run due to the qualitative superiority of the Israel military, one should not rule out a Syrian assault against Israel. The objective of trying to restore the Golan by force could be to mobilize public support for the regime if it reaches a serious state of domestic vulnerability. After all, the Syrian military build-up with Scud missiles does not signal a retreat from confrontation with Israel. Rather, it underscores the danger of a future war that, despite its almost certain military outcome, could inflict heavy casualties on Israel and reshuffle the political cards in the region.

Lebanon

In the foreseeable future, Lebanon's government is most unlikely to deviate from Syria's policy of a comprehensive Middle Eastern settlement; hence, its talks with Israel are unlikely to come to fruition before a real breakthrough takes place in the Israeli-Syrian negotiations. Lebanon is committed, however, to UN Resolution 425, which calls for the withdrawal of Israeli forces from south Lebanon. Israel will not implement that resolution until it receives satisfactory security assurances through negotiations, which may also require a peace treaty similar to that made in May 1983, which former President Gemayel later repudiated. A resolution of the issue of water sharing, which is one of the subjects in the multilateral peace talks, might also be linked to a final peace agreement between the two states.

CONCLUSION

Desert Storm has exacerbated the prewar instability of several Arab regimes, the legitimacy of which has been increasingly questioned by their citizens. The sources of instability are many. High population growth, authoritarian or oligarchic leadership, and economic stagnation by themselves pose severe strains on political stability. Yet more unsettling is the rise of Islamist-dominated political oppositions, including some militant, uncompromising groups, the continuation of the conflict over the Palestinian question, and the persistence or deepening of a number of bilateral disputes.

The Gulf War served both to tip the balance of military power in the Middle East heavily in Israel's favor and to dispel two longstanding myths among Arabs: one, that Arab states had the ability to achieve military parity with Israel as a prelude to regaining the occupied territories; and two, that pan-Arab solidarity would inevitably surface when one or more Arab countries engaged in a conflict with a non-Arab power.

As the forces of social, economic, and political destabilization continue to plague their countries, Arabs are realizing that maintaining the present status quo truly is more "dangerous than a potential negotiated compromise."[29] All members of the Arab League now endorse UN Resolutions 242 and 338. Furthermore, more than two years after the beginning of the Gulf War, the Arab states and the PLO continue to negotiate with Israel with the objective of restoring at least part of the occupied territories prior to reaching a peace accord. The negotiation process may stop if domestic opposition—chiefly from Islamic militants—grows significantly. The nature of the peace proposals will play a large part in determining whether negotiations with Israel receive the endorsement not only of the Arab governments but also of their peoples.

The United States is expected to formulate these proposals, market them, and provide incentives and disincentives to the participants. Other parties, such as Egypt, Saudi Arabia, the European Community, and Japan, can certainly play important facilitating roles, but in the post–Cold War and post–Gulf War world, the final arbiter and guarantor of the proposed resolution/settlement can only be the United States. Without its active involvement at the highest level, the multilayered peace process is unlikely to proceed to a successful conclusion.

Appendix A

Selected Demographic Indicators for the Arab Countries

Country	Population (in millions, 1992)	Area ('000s of square kilometers)	Urban Population (% of total population, 1990)	Total Fertility Rate (per woman, 1990–1995)	Annual Rate of Change (%, 1990–1995)
Algeria	26.3	2,382	52	4.9	2.7
Bahrain	0.5	691	83	3.7	2.8
Egypt	54.8	1,001	44	4.1	2.2
Iraq	19.3	438	72	5.7	3.2
Jordan	4.3	89	68	5.7	3.4
Kuwait	2.0	18	96	3.7	–5.8
Lebanon	3.7*	10	84	3.1	2.0
Libya	4.9	1,760	82	6.4	3.5
Mauritania	2.1	1,026	47	6.5	2.9
Morocco	26.3	447	46	4.4	2.4
Oman	1.6	212	11	6.7	3.6
Qatar	0.4	11	90	4.4	2.8
Saudi Arabia	15.9	2,150	77	6.4	3.4
Somalia	9.2	638	24	7.0	3.2
Sudan	26.6	2,506	23	6.0	2.8
Syria	13.3	185	50	6.1	3.6
Tunisia	8.4	164	56	3.4	2.1
United Arab Emirates	1.7	84	81	4.5	2.3
Yemen	12.5	528	29	7.2	3.5
West Bank and Gaza	1.8*	7	94**	6.3*	2.0**

* Figures estimated by author based on UN-ESCWA, *Demographic and Socioeconomic Data Sheets 1988* (Baghdad: ESCWA, 1989).

** Gaza Strip only.

Sources: United Nations, *World Population Prospects: The 1992 Revision;* United Nations, *World Population 1992.*

Appendix B

Selected Socioeconomic Indicators for the Arab Countries

Country	Adult Illiteracy (%, 1990)	GNP per Capita ($100s, 1990)	Life Expectancy at Birth (years, 1990–1995)	Infant Mortality (per 1,000, 1990–1995)
Algeria	43	21	66.2	61
Bahrain	23	102**	71.2	12
Egypt	52	6	61.6	57
Iraq	40	n/a	66.0	58
Jordan	20	12	67.9	36
Kuwait	27	161***	74.7	14
Lebanon	20	n/a	68.5	34
Libya	36	53***	63.1	68
Mauritania	66	5	48.0	117
Morocco	50	9	63.3	68
Oman	n/a	52***	69.6	30
Qatar	24	n/a	70.0	26
Saudi Arabia	38	70	69.2	31
Somalia	76	1	47.0	122
Sudan	73	n/a	51.8	99
Syria	35	10	67.1	39
Tunisia	35	14	67.8	43
United Arab Emirates	30*	199	71.2	22
Yemen	61	6	52.7	106
West Bank and Gaza	20*	n/a	67.9	36*

n/a—not available.

* Figures estimated by author based on UN-ESCWA, *Demographic and Socioeconomic Data Sheets 1988* (Baghdad: ESCWA, 1989).

** For 1987.

*** For 1989.

Sources: United Nations, *World Population Prospects: The 1992 Revision;* The World Bank, *World Development Report 1992;* UNESCO, *Statistical Yearbook, 1991.*

Notes

Chapter 1

1. The simultaneous use of the words "Arabian" and "Persian" reflects the author's neutrality in the dispute between the Arab countries bordering the Gulf and Iran over whether the so-called Persian Gulf is a Persian or an Arab territory. To avoid this messy expression without sacrificing the author's neutrality, the Arabian/Persian Gulf will, hereafter, be referred to as the Gulf.

2. The Arab states are Algeria, Bahrain, Djibouti, Egypt, Iraq, Jordan, Kuwait, Lebanon, Libya, Mauritania, Morocco, Oman, Qatar, Saudi Arabia, Somalia, Sudan, Syria, Tunisia, the United Arab Emirates, and Yemen.

3. Carl Brown, "Patterns Forged in Time: Middle Eastern Mindsets and the Gulf War" (Paper delivered at the Conference on the Political Psychology of the Gulf War: Leaders, Publics and the Process of Conflict, City University of New York, November 11–12, 1991), 5.

4. For more figures and further details, see appendix A.

5. The World Bank classifies countries of the world into income categories, the highest of which is the "upper-income" group. Each country in this group has a gross national product per capita that exceeds $2,400. Presently, the upper-income Arab states are Bahrain, Kuwait, Libya, Oman, Qatar, Saudi Arabia, and the United Arab Emirates. Until 1980 Iraq was part of this group, but even then the populations of the upper-income Arab countries combined made up less than 15 percent of the total Arab population.

6. Statistical data are presented in appendix B.

7. Estimates of the number of Berbers in the Maghreb vary widely, ranging from 15 to 20 percent of the population in Algeria and about twice that in Morocco. For details, see Minority Rights Group, ed., *World Directory of Minorities* (Essex, England: Longman International Reference, 1990), 184–86.

8. Brown, "Patterns Forged in Time," 8–10.

9. Alan Taylor, *The Arab Balance of Power System* (Syracuse, N.Y.: Syracuse University Press, 1982), 4–6.

10. Brown, "Patterns Forged in Time," 8–10.

11. Alexander George, "The Gulf War: Possible Impact on the International System" (Paper presented at the Conference on the Political Psychology of the Gulf War: Leaders, Publics and the Process of Conflict, City University of New York, November 11–12, 1991), 1.

12. Ibid., 2.

13. Ibid., 4.

14. Samuel P. Huntington, "How Countries Democratize," *Political Science Quarterly* 106, no. 4 (Winter 1991–92): 579.

15. Ibid., the footnote to table 1, 582.

16. See, for example, Robert L. Rothstein, "Democracy, Conflict, and Development in the Third World," *Washington Quarterly* (Spring 1991): 43.

17. Ibid., 47. See also Rudolph Rummel, "Libertarianism and International Violence," *Journal of Conflict Resolution,* no. 27 (March 1983): 27–71.

18. Rothstein, "Democracy, Conflict, and Development," 43, 53–56.

19. Known oil reserves in the world, as of December 1991, amount to 991 billion barrels, of which 600 billion (over 60 percent) are in the Arab world. Oil reserves (in billions of barrels) of selected countries are distributed as follows: Saudi Arabia 260.3, Iraq 100.0, Kuwait 96.5, Algeria 9.2, Egypt 4.5. See *Oil and Gas Journal,* December 30, 1991.

Chapter 2

1. An explanation of the author's methodology appears in chapter 1.

2. The lower estimate was given by the air commander Lieutenant-General Charles A. Horner in an interview with Cable News Network (CNN) on January 14, 1992. The upper estimate, with at least 50 percent margin of error, made by the Defense Intelligence Agency, was reported in *The Washington Post,* January 16, 1992, A10.

3. A study by the United States House Armed Services Committee that relied on interviews of Iraqi prisoners estimated that about 9,000 Iraqi soldiers perished from air assaults. According to the Iraqi government, some 7,000 civilians also died in those assaults. A much higher figure was given by senior U.S. military officials of between 60,000 and 80,000 (*Middle East Report* 21, no. 171 [July/August 1991]: 4).

4. *The Washington Post,* March 6, 1992, A6.

5. Ibid.

6. *Middle East Report* 21, no. 171 (July/August 1991): 4–5. This magazine puts the range of casualties at 100,000 to 200,000.

7. Dilip Hiro, *The Longest War: The Iran-Iraq Military Conflict* (New York: Routledge, 1991), 250.

8. *Mideast Mirror,* October 22, 1991, 24.

9. *Foreign Broadcast Information Service (FBIS) Daily Report: Near East and South Asia,* June 23, 1992, 31.

10. Although various sources of data on the numbers of foreigners in Iraq before August 2, 1990, are consistent regarding the numbers of Europeans and Americans, they are inconsistent with regard to estimates of other foreigners. The figures the author has used lie in the middle range of estimates given in the following sources: *The New York Times,* December 7 and September 22, 1990; *The Economist,* September 8, 1990; *Time,* August 27, 1990; and Europa Publications, *The Europa Year Book 1991* (London: Europa Publications, 1991).

11. Refugee figures are from United Nations High Commissioner for Refugees, *Information Bulletin* 6 (October 3, 1991): 3–4, 7–8.

12. This information was given in the U.S. Senate report issued in January 1992 and the United Nations High Commissioner for Refugees, *Information Bulletin* 6 (January 27, 1992): 3.

13. United Nations High Commissioner for Refugees, *Information Bulletin* 8 (January 27, 1992): 8.

14. Ibid., 6.

15. Europa Publications, *The Middle East and North Africa 1992* (London: Europa Publications, 1992), 497.

16. Ibid., 504.

17. Ibid., 505.

18. Ibrahim M. Oweiss, "Economic Impact of the Gulf War with Special Reference to the Economies of Selected Arab Countries" (Unpublished manuscript, Georgetown University, 1992), 8.

19. Elizabeth N. Offen, "The Persian Gulf War of 1990/1991: Its Impact on Migration and the Security of States" (Unpublished manuscript, MIT Department of Political Science, December 1991), 24.

20. Oweiss, "Economic Impact," 8.

21. *The Middle East and North Africa 1992,* 497.

22. Iraq has refused to sell its oil according to UN terms under which some 30 percent of the revenues would be used to pay for war reparations, compensation claims, and costs of UN missions in Iraq. According to The Economist Intelligence Unit (its *Iraq, Country Report,* no. 1 [1992]: 14), much of Iraq's recalcitrance is due to its inability to export oil. Before the Gulf War, the Turkish pipeline was the main route for export. Reopening it now brings little financial benefit for two reasons: First, Turkey is demanding a very high price; and second, the Kurds control an 80-kilometer stretch of the pipeline and are able to sabotage it at other points. The alternative export route is Mina al-Bakr on the Gulf, which, although the Iraqis claim to have repaired it, still needs engineering work on the north-south pipeline before it can be operational. Repair will require replacement parts, which Iraq is not allowed to import under the present terms of UN economic sanctions.

23. The Economist Intelligence Unit, *Iraq, Country Report*, no. 1 (1992): 14.

24. Ibid., 12. See also *The Middle East and North Africa 1992*, 498.

25. The Economist Intelligence Unit, *Iraq, Country Report*, no. 2 (1992): 13, and no. 3 (1992): 19–20.

26. Figures are from ibid., 13–15. See also *The New York Times*, July 14, 1992, A6.

27. Figures are from Middle East Watch, which cites, among other sources of information, a cardiologist who used to work in one of the main hospitals in Kuwait and a senior official in the then-Kuwaiti government-in-exile. For further details, see Middle East Watch, "Kuwait: Deteriorating Human Rights Conditions Since the Early Occupation," *News from the Middle East*, November 16, 1990, 6–8.

28. This figure, reported in the state-run newspaper *Sawt al-Kuwait* on April 1, 1992, was given by the acting head of Kuwait's delegation to the Arab League.

29. Estimates of killings vary by source. For example, whereas the PLO spokesman in Tunis estimated that over 300 Palestinians were killed in Kuwait, an officer from the then-PLO embassy in Kuwait gave a more plausible toll: over 37 Palestinians and Jordanians killed by the end of May 1991 (Middle East Watch, *A Victory Turned Sour: Human Rights in Kuwait Since Liberation* [New York: Human Rights Watch, September 1991], 13, footnote 49).

30. Ibid., 7–13. Also, Dean Fischer of *Time* magazine placed the number of Palestinians killed at the hands of Kuwaiti resistance fighters at 100 (*Time*, January 27, 1992, 28).

31. This discussion of the Palestinians in Kuwait is based on a draft report about the Palestinian refugees by Don Peretz. The report was presented at the United States Institute of Peace, Washington, D.C., April 1992. See also Don Peretz, *Palestinians, Refugees, and the Middle East Peace Process* (Washington, D.C.: United States Institute of Peace Press, 1993).

32. See the Peretz draft report, 27. In Peretz's judgment, about 10 percent of the Palestinians collaborated with the occupiers, another 10 percent assisted the Kuwaiti resistance, and the rest merely followed Iraqi orders.

For more details about the relations between Palestinians and Kuwaitis during the occupation, see Shafiq Ghabra, "The Iraqi Occupation of Kuwait: An Eyewitness Account," *Journal of Palestine Studies* 20, no. 2 (Winter 1991): 112–25. See also Milton Viorst, "A Reporter at Large: After the Liberation," *New Yorker*, September 30, 1991, 37–72.

33. *Mideast Mirror*, February 3, 1992, 10–11.

34. Middle East Watch, *A Victory Turned Sour*, 46–48.

35. *Mideast Mirror*, May 12, 1992, 15.

36. *Mideast Mirror*, January 28, 1992, 25–26.

37. This figure was communicated in a telephone conversation between the author's assistant, Paula Bailey-Smith, and the Kuwait Desk Officer in early May 1992.

38. Estimate by Ahmad al-Jassar, Kuwait's minister of planning (*Mideast Mirror*, January 15, 1992, 2).

39. According to PLO chairman Yasir Arafat in an interview with the Middle East Broadcasting Center, aired July 28, 1992. However, at the end of May 1992, Hamad al-Jassar of *Sawt al-Kuwait* estimated the number of remaining Palestinians at 20,000 to 25,000, 60 percent of whose applications for extension of stay were turned down (*Mideast Mirror*, June 2, 1992, 22).

40. This is an unofficial figure that was obtained from the Kuwaiti Ministry of Planning by Middle East Watch (*A Victory Turned Sour,* 51).

41. See ibid.

42. Ibid., 53–54.

43. Based on an article in *Sawt al-Kuwait*, as cited in *Mideast Mirror*, January 28, 1992, 26.

44. Oweiss, "Economic Impact," 9, cites Abdullah Dabbagh, secretary general of Saudi Arabia's Chamber of Commerce, as estimating the war damage at no more than $20 billion, which is very close to the U.S. State Department's estimate of $20 to $25 billion.

45. Assuming a constant price per barrel of $16 and the 1990 level of production, 2.04 million barrels a day.

46. Estimated and actual oil production and revenues are drawn from The Economist Intelligence Unit, *Kuwait, Country Report*, no. 1 (1992): 5; no. 3 (1992): 5; and no. 1 (1993): 6.

47. A U.S. State Department figure.

48. Figure provided by the Kuwaiti minister of finance (*Mideast Mirror*, November 13, 1991, 24).

49. *Sawt al-Kuwait*, May 12, 1992.

50. *The New York Times*, May 6, 1992, A4.

51. The Economist Intelligence Unit, *Kuwait, Country Report*, no. 1 (1992): 9.

52. *Mideast Mirror*, May 11, 1992, 19.

53. Youssef M. Ibrahim, "Rulers of Kuwait on Spending Spree, Raising Debt Fears," *The New York Times*, May 4, 1992, A1, A6.

54. The Economist Intelligence Unit, *Kuwait, Country Report*, no. 1 (1993): 6.

55. Some government sources in Jordan estimate the prewar percentage of Palestinians in the East Bank at 40 percent (Ellen Laipson and Alfred Prados, *Jordan: Recent Developments and Implications for U.S. Interests*, CRS Report for Congress [Washington, D.C.: CRS, July 11, 1990], 3).

56. Estimate by the author based on projecting the United Nations–Economic and Social Commission for Western Asia's (UN-ESCWA) estimate for 1988, which is 2.82 million.

57. Reported by The Economist Intelligence Unit, *Jordan, Country Report*, no. 1 (1992): 21–22.

58. Estimate by Oweiss, "Economic Impact," 14; and The Economist Intelligence Unit, *Jordan, Country Profile 1992–93*: 13.

59. *Mideast Mirror*, May 6, 1992, 10, citing the Shipping Agents Association of Jordan as its source.

60. Estimate by the United Nations, Social and Economic Council, as cited in Oweiss, "Economic Impact," 6.

61. The Economist Intelligence Unit, *Jordan, Country Report*, no. 2 (1992): 4; and *Jordan, Country Profile 1992–93*: 16.

62. *The New York Times*, October 3, 1991, A10, citing Jordanian authorities as the source.

63. *The New York Times*, September 19, 1991, A18.

64. Yahya Sadowski, "Arab Economies after the Gulf War: Power, Poverty, and Petrodollars," *Middle East Report* 170 (May/June 1991): 10.

65. Europa Publications, *The Middle East and North Africa 1992*, 586.

66. The Economist Intelligence Unit, *Jordan, Country Report*, no. 1 (1993): 6.

67. Ibid., 7.

68. Ibid., 4, and The Economist Intelligence Unit, *Jordan, Country Report*, no. 3 (1992): 4.

69. The Economist Intelligence Unit, *Jordan, Country Report*, no. 3 (1992): 4–5, 16–22.

70. Sadowski, "Arab Economies," 10.

71. Officials in the Saudi embassy in Washington, D.C., said in late 1992 that they had no figures.

72. Offen, "The Persian Gulf War," 26.

73. Reported in *The New York Times*, June 16, 1991.

74. Oweiss, "Economic Impact," 14.

75. Ibid., 11, based on a letter from the Saudi ambassador to the United States, dated January 24, 1991.

76. Oweiss, "Economic Impact," 10.

77. *Asharq al-Awsat*, January 2, 1992, as cited in *Mideast Mirror*, January 3, 1992, 16.

78. Source of figure is the U.S. Defense Department.

79. *Mideast Mirror*, September 24, 1991, 19.

80. For more details, see The Economist Intelligence Unit, *Saudi Arabia, Country Report*, no. 1 (1992): 14–15; and *Mideast Mirror*, January 3, 1992, 16.

81. *Mideast Mirror*, March 25, 1992, 8–9.

82. The Economist Intelligence Unit, *Saudi Arabia, Country Report*, no. 1 (1993): 5.

83. Oweiss, "Economic Impact," 13.

84. *Mideast Mirror*, September 24, 1991, 19.

85. Europa Publications, *The Middle East and North Africa 1992*, 402.

86. The Economist Intelligence Unit, *Egypt, Country Report*, no. 2 (1992): 6.

87. The Economist Intelligence Unit, *Egypt, Country Report*, no. 3 (1992): 4.

88. Ibid., 5.

89. See The Economist Intelligence Unit, *Egypt, Country Report*, no. 1 (1992): 10–11.

90. The Economist Intelligence Unit, *Egypt, Country Report*, no. 3 (1992): 4.

Chapter 3

1. Michael C. Hudson, "After the Gulf War: Prospects for Democratization in the Arab World," *Middle East Journal* 45, no. 3 (1991): 407–26.

2. Much of this chapter is based on an earlier, less comprehensive article by this author, titled "Democracy and the Arab World: A Study of Four Countries."

3. See Albert P. Blaustein and Gilbert H. Flanz, eds., *Constitutions of the Countries of the World* (New York: Oceana Publications, 1990).

4. The Jordanian National Charter, version distributed by the Jordanian Embassy in Washington, D.C., chapter 2, section 1.

5. See Herodotus, *The Histories*, A. de Selincourt, trans. (Middlesex, England: Penguin, 1984).

6. Aristotle, *The Politics of Aristotle*, E. Barker, trans., rev. ed. (Oxford: Clarendon, 1961), 164.

7. See Robert A. Dahl, *Polyarchy: Participation and Opposition* (New Haven, Conn., and London: Yale University Press, 1971).

8. Robert A. Dahl, *Democracy and Its Critics* (New Haven, Conn., and London: Yale University Press, 1989), 108–31.

9. Ibid.

10. See Giovanni Sartori, *Democratic Theory* (New York: Praeger, 1965).

11. See Ted R. Gurr, Keith Jaggers, and Will H. Moore, *Polity II Handbook* (Boulder, Colo.: University of Colorado, 1989).

12. Ibid. See also Zeev Maoz and Bruce Russett, "Alliances, Contiguity, Wealth, and Political Stability: Is the Lack of Conflict among Democracies a Statistical Artifact?" (Paper delivered at the Annual Meeting of the American Political Science Association, San Francisco, August 30–September 2, 1990).

13. Indicators of democracy are even more diverse than its definitions. This is due, in part, to the failure of scholars to agree on a unified conceptualization of the dimensions of a democratic order. Yet, measures and scales of democracy largely agree in their classification of UN member states into democratic and nondemocratic categories. Different scales do not yield the same results for the same Arab countries, but they are unanimous in considering all the Arab states nonpolyarchic. For further details, see Muhammad Faour, "Democracy and the Arab World: A Study of Four Countries."

14. For example, see Hudson, "After the Gulf War," and John L. Esposito and James P. Piscatori, "Democratization and Islam," *Middle East Journal* 45, no. 3 (1991): 427–40.

15. The concept of a consultative body is based on *shura*, which is upheld by all Muslims.

16. Boudiaf, the assassinated head of the Algerian High Committee of State, vowed repeatedly to punish corrupt officials "whatever their social position or hierarchical rank," requesting new legislation to that effect (as quoted by Jonathan Randal, *The Washington Post*, July 1, 1992, A25). Some officials and army generals are accused of accepting large commissions on contraband trade and arms purchases. The first Algerian president after independence, Ahmad Ben Bella, accused the regime under Benjedid of embezzling $15 billion from the state treasury, a charge that Benjedid categorically denied. An opinion poll published in March 1992 showed that nearly 30 percent of the Algerian respondents believed that prosperity in the country was contingent on ending corruption (*Mideast Mirror*, March 23, 1992, 24).

17. Boudiaf was assassinated on June 29, 1992.

18. According to government officials, the number of Islamists detained in the desert camps during Boudiaf's term reached at least 7,683 (*The Washington Post*, July 1, 1992, A26).

19. Ibid., A22. Between January and June 1992, over 55 people were killed in the clashes between the Algerian armed forces and Islamist protesters.

20. *Mideast Mirror*, March 23, 1992, 24.

21. *The Washington Post*, July 1, 1992, A26.

22. Nazih N. Ayubi, "Domestic Politics," in Lilian C. Harris, ed., *Egypt: Internal Challenges and Regional Stability* (New York: Routledge and Kegan Paul, 1988), 75–76.

23. Ibid.

24. *Mideast Mirror*, December 5, 1991, 12.

25. *Mideast Mirror*, November 29, 1990, 22–25.

26. Reported in the *Mideast Mirror*, November 28, 1990, 13.

27. Raymond D. Gastil, *Freedom in the World: Political Rights and Civil Liberties, 1990–1991* (New York: Freedom House, 1991), 150–52.

28. See Blaustein and Flanz, *Constitutions.*

29. Europa Publications, *The Europa Year Book 1991*, 1536–40.

30. There are several indicators of Jordan's assertive politics: (1) the government's rejection in June 1992 of the 'Aqaba Plus proposal by the Bush administration, which called for the stationing of UN observers in Jordan to stop the contraband trade between Jordan and Iraq; (2) Jordan's unshaken stance toward assuming responsibility for restoration of the Islamic holy places in East Jerusalem, in rivalry with Saudi Arabia, which had also decided to pay the restoration costs via UNESCO; and (3) King Hussein's refusal to apologize to the Saudis for his stance during the Gulf crisis (see chapter 5).

31. Europa Publications, *The Europa Year Book 1991*, 225, 1536–40.

32. The Jordanian National Charter, 17.

33. Blaustein and Flanz, *Constitutions*, 33–37.

34. For details and further analysis, see *Ash-shiraa*, no. 533 (November 23, 1992): 30–31.

35. Virginia N. Sherry, "What the Democratic Forces Want," *The Nation*, November 5, 1990, 528.

36. Ibid., 526.

37. For details, see *al-Hayat*, October 8, 1992, 7.

38. The electorate number was officially announced by the government daily *Sawt al-Kuwait*, March 27, 1992. The number of Kuwaitis is estimated by the author as a projection of the 1988 estimate made by UN-ESCWA, Amman, Jordan.

39. In essence, the statutes make up a constitution, but the term *constitution* is constantly avoided in Saudi politics because of its possible misinterpretation by the highly restrictive school of Wahhabis that provides the religious, ideological legitimacy for the monarchy. The king has asserted countless times that these statutes are not a constitution since the Saudi state is founded on *shari'a*, which is based on the Koran and the Sunna.

40. Reported in the *Mideast Mirror*, March 30, 1992, 12.

41. In December 1990, 43 public figures representing both religious and secular orientations signed a petition addressed to the king, proposing 10 reforms: notably, a basic law of government, a consultative council, equality among citizens, establishment of rules that specify the mandate of the religious police, and improvement of the status of women. Two months later, the clergy, led by Sheikh Bin Baz, submitted another petition that not only concurred with the first petition on the consultative council and rights of individuals, but also emphasized the traditional missionary role of the kingdom and stated that all laws must conform to the *shari'a*. For further details, see Middle East Watch, *Empty Reforms: Saudi Arabia's New Basic Laws* (New York: Human Rights Watch, May 1992), 59–62.

42. Gastil, *Freedom in the World*, 321–22.

43. Philippe Schmitter, "Society," in National Research Council, *The Transition to Democracy: Proceedings of a Workshop* (Washington, D.C.: National Academy Press, 1991), 16–25.

44. Samuel P. Huntington, "Will More Countries Become Democratic?" in Samuel Huntington and Joseph Nye, Jr., eds., *Global Dilemmas* (Cambridge, Mass.: Harvard University Press, 1985), 253–79.

45. See Albert Hourani, *A History of the Arab Peoples* (Cambridge, Mass.: Harvard University Press, 1991).

46. Ibid., 449.

47. See Leonard Binder, *In a Moment of Enthusiasm: Political Power and the Second Stratum* (Chicago: University of Chicago Press, 1978); and Hamid Ansari, *Egypt: The Stalled Society* (Albany, N.Y.: State University of New York Press, 1986).

48. British Broadcasting Corporation (BBC), Summary of World Broadcasts, Middle East and Africa, April 6, 1987, A/10.

49. Hanna Batatu, "Political Power and Social Structure in Syria and Iraq," in Samih Farsoun, ed., *Arab Society: Continuity and Change* (London: Croom Helm, 1985), 34–47.

50. Ibid.

51. The 1989 riots staged by Bedouin and native Jordanians in the southern cities of Jordan, particularly Ma'an, were no exception. They were not directed against the king but rather against the economic policies of the government. After making this conclusion, the king did not alter the social composition of his Bedouin-dominated army, despite his dismay at the Bedouin upheaval.

52. Giacomo Luciani and Hazem Beblawi, *The Rentier State* (London: Croom Helm, 1987); and Yezid Sayigh, "The Gulf Crisis: Why the Arab Regional Order Failed," *International Affairs* 67, no. 3 (1991): 487–507.

53. Ibid. See also Batatu, "Political Power."

54. F. Gregory Gause, "Sovereignty, Statecraft and Stability in the Middle East" (Paper delivered at the Annual Meeting of the American Political Science Association, Washington, D.C., August 29–September 1, 1984), table 2 on page 13.

55. Quantitative estimates for Egypt and Iraq are provided by Hanna Batatu, "The Egyptian, Syrian and Iraqi Revolutions: Some Observations on Their Underlying Causes and Social Character" (Inaugural lecture given at Center for Contemporary Arab Studies, Georgetown University, January 25, 1983).

56. Hisham Sharabi, "The Dialectics of Patriarchy in Arab Society," in Farsoun, ed., *Arab Society*, 83–104.

57. Schmitter, "Society," 16–25.

58. Huntington, "Will More Countries Become Democratic?"

59. This view, though bleak, is shared by a number of eminent scholars. For instance, in a personal interview with this author on June 17, 1992, Professor Halim Barakat of Georgetown University contended that the Arab regimes have destroyed civil society in their countries.

60. Huntington, "Will More Countries Become Democratic?"

61. *The Holy Koran*, particularly suras 3 and 42 (3:159 and 42:38).

62. See Fahmi Jadaane, "Notions of the State in Contemporary Arab-Islamic Writings," in Ghassan Salamé, ed., *The Foundations of the Arab State* (London: Croom Helm, 1987), 141–42.

63. In Egypt, for instance, the religious views of al-Azhar and the Muslim Brotherhood prevail over the fundamentalist views of the militant Islamic movements.

64. Huntington, "Will More Countries Become Democratic?"

65. Ibid., for details.

66. Dahl, *Democracy and Its Critics*, 264.

67. See Leonard Binder, *Islamic Liberalism: A Critique of Development Ideologies* (Chicago: Chicago University Press, 1989).

Chapter 4

1. Morroe Berger, *The Arab World Today* (New York: Doubleday & Company, Inc., 1962), 323.

2. For details of the Hussein-McMahon correspondence and conversations, see Elie Keddourie, *In the Anglo-Arab Labyrinth: The McMahon-Husayn Correspondence and Its Interpretations, 1914–1939* (Cambridge, England: Cambridge University Press, 1976).

3. Tareq Ismael and Jacqueline Ismael, "The Legacy of Nationalism," chapter 4 in Tareq Ismael and Jacqueline Ismael, eds., *Politics and Government in the Middle East and North Africa* (Miami: Florida International University Press, 1991).

4. Michael N. Barnett, "Sovereignty, Institutions, and Identity: From Pan-Arabism to the Arab State System" (Paper delivered at the 1991 Annual Meeting of the American Political Science Association, Washington, D.C., August 29–September 1, 1991).

5. Internal sovereignty refers to the state's legitimate role as the highest authority in domestic affairs, and external authority is a recognition by the world that a state is independent from all other states.

6. Bassam Tibi, "The Simultaneity of the Unsimultaneous: Old Tribes and Imposed Nation-States in the Modern Middle East," in Philip Khoury and Joseph Kostiner, eds., *Tribes and State Formation in the Middle East* (Berkeley, Calif.: University of California Press, 1990), 127–52.

7. Anthony Giddens, *The Nation-State and Violence* (Berkeley, Calif.: University of California Press, 1987), 210.

8. See Abul A'la al-Mawdudi, *Islamic Way of Life*, 11th ed. (Lahore, Pakistan: Islamic Publications, 1979).

9. Ismael and Ismael, "The Legacy of Nationalism," 68.

10. Detailed examples from Egypt, Iraq, Syria, Jordan, and the Maghreb were provided by Amatzia Baram, "Territorial Nationalism in the Middle East," *Middle Eastern Studies* (London) 26, no. 4 (October 1990), 425–48.

11. Barnett, "Sovereignty, Institutions," 13.

12. Taylor, *The Arab Balance*, 23.

13. Iliya Harik, "The Origins of the Arab State System," in Ghassan Salamé, ed., *The Foundations of the Arab State* (London: Croom Helm, 1987), 45.

14. Syria seceded from Egypt in 1961 after a three-year period of unification. Egypt under Nasser, and Syria and Iraq under the Ba'ath failed to unite in 1963, despite their common ideology of pan-Arabism. Libya failed to establish union with any of the Arab states to which it proposed unity. The only exception is the union of the two Yemens, but it is still too early to give a final judgment as to whether or not the union will be permanent.

15. See Ali al-Wardi, *Shakhsiyyat al-Fard al-'Iraqi* (The personality of the Iraqi individual) (Baghdad: al-Rabita Press, 1951).

16. Albert Hourani, *Syria and Lebanon* (London: Oxford University Press, 1946), 71–72.

17. Hourani, *A History of the Arab Peoples*, 455.

18. Sydney N. Fisher and William Ochsenwald, *The Middle East: A History*, 4th ed. (New York: McGraw-Hill, Inc., 1990), 738–39.

19. "Myth" here refers to the group belief or collective self-image among Arabs that is based on a selective reading of their history.

20. Brown, "Patterns Forged in Time," 10–11.

21. Fisher and Ochsenwald, *The Middle East*, 736.

22. Fundamentalism is defined here as the strict adherence to the letter of the *shari'a* and its rigid, constrictive interpretation.

23. See James Piscatori, "Religion and Realpolitik: Islamic Responses to the Gulf War," in James Piscatori, ed., *Islamic Fundamentalisms and the Gulf Crisis* (Chicago: Academy of Arts and Sciences, 1992), 9.

24. The Arab feeling of defeat is based on the contention that the Iraqi army and its weaponry belong to the Arab nation as a whole—irrespective of the nature of the Iraqi regime. Therefore, the defeat of the Iraqi army and the destruction of its weaponry were viewed as losses to the Arabs as a nation. Had Saddam not invaded Kuwait, these Iraqi—and thus Arab—assets would have been spared, and the overall military power of the Arabs would have been greater.

25. Hourani, *A History of the Arab Peoples*, 457–58.

26. In the case of Saudi Arabia, the regime itself is fundamentalist Islamic but is challenged by more puritanical groups whose popular influence and organizational strength are yet to be determined for want of accurate information.

27. Caryle Murphy, "Islam: Politics and Piety, Part I," *The Washington Post*, April 26, 1992, A28.

28. There has been speculation within the United States that Sheikh Abdul Rahman was involved, either directly or indirectly, in the bombing of the World Trade Center in New York City in February 1993.

29. This information appeared in an article by Salaheddin Hafez, assistant editor of *al-Ahram*, and was cited in *Mideast Mirror*, May 27, 1992, 21.

30. Farag Foda, a secularist writer and staunch opponent of Islamic fundamentalism, was assassinated by Islamic militants in Cairo in June 1992.

31. See *Civil Society* newsletter (Cairo, Ibn Khaldoun Center for Development Studies, January 1992), no. 1, 20.

32. The Azhar is the most distinguished academy of higher learning in Sunni Islam. It is a traditional, conservative body that has continuously played a legitimating role for the Egyptian regime and its policies. For many years, the successive rulers of Egypt maintained a distinct policy toward the Azhar. They have patronized this institution and made it part of their bureaucracy.

33. *Mideast Mirror,* April 1, 1992, 16.

34. Chris Hedges, "A Religious War Rends a Cairo Slum," *The New York Times*, October 22, 1991, A12; and *Mideast Mirror*, September 24, 1991, 15.

35. *Mideast Mirror* (May 6, 1992, 13) reported that the clashes followed a three-month dispute between a Christian and a Muslim family over a property sale. The dispute led to a fight that resulted in three deaths. The following month a Christian was killed in an apparent revenge for one of the Muslims killed earlier.

36. This charge is also made by the Coptic associations in the United States, Canada, and Australia in their repeated advertisements (see note 42 below).

37. *Mideast Mirror*, May 27, 1992, 22.

38. Hedges, "A Religious War."

39. Ghali Shukri, as cited in *Mideast Mirror*, May 27, 1992, 23.

40. According to Egyptian government estimates, Copts make up 10 percent of the population, or under 6 million, while Coptic associations in the West put the number of Copts at 11 million, or 20 percent of the total population.

41. Murphy, "Islam: Politics and Piety," A29.

42. *Mideast Mirror,* May 27, 1992, 22. The same advertisement was repeatedly published in *The New York Times*, for instance, on June 25, 1992, A12.

43. The phrase was stated by Sa'deddin Ibrahim (see Murphy, "Islam: Politics and Piety," A28).

44. This explanation is based on the frustration-aggression theory in social psychology. See Lawrence Berkowitz, "Frustration-Aggression Hypothesis," *Psychological Bulletin* 106 (1989): 59-73; Lawrence Berkowitz, *A Survey of Social Psychology*, 2nd ed. (New York: Holt, Rinehart and Winston, 1979); and Albert Bandura, *Social Learning Theory* (Englewood Cliffs, N.J.: Prentice-Hall, 1977).

45. For further details, see chapter 5.

46. As confirmed by Adnan Abu Owdeh, Jordan's ambassador to the United Nations and former longtime adviser to King Hussein, in his talk at the symposium on "Islam and Democracy," which was sponsored by the United States Institute of Peace in Washington, D.C., May 15, 1992.

47. Beverley Milton-Edwards, "A Temporary Alliance with the Crown: the Islamic Response in Jordan," in Piscatori, *Islamic Fundamentalisms*, 92-94.

48. Ibid., 105-6.

49. *Mideast Mirror*, October 29, 1991, 13-14.

50. *Mideast Mirror*, November 1, 1991, 20.

51. *Mideast Mirror*, October 14, 1991, 15. A translated text of the king's speech appears on pages 14-19.

52. *Mideast Mirror*, November 22, 1991, 12.

53. Ibid.

54. Ibid., 13.

55. *Mideast Mirror*, December 2, 1991, 3-4.

56. *Mideast Mirror*, December 5, 1991, 9.

57. Caryle Murphy, "Islam: Politics and Piety, Part II," *The Washington Post*, April 27, 1992, A16.

58. *Mideast Mirror*, May 7, 1992, 23.

59. *Mideast Mirror*, May 18, 1992, 18.

60. *Mideast Mirror*, May 26, 1992, 26.

61. For further details, see Hugh Roberts, "A Trial of Strength: Algerian Islamism," in Piscatori, ed., *Islamic Fundamentalisms*, 133-38.

62. Ibid., 138-39.

63. See Algeria's country report prepared by the Freedom House Survey Team, in Gastil, *Freedom in the World*, 61-64.

64. Roberts, "A Trial of Strength," 149.

65. Usama Aggag wrote for *Sawt al-Kuwait* and was cited in *Mideast Mirror*, October 23, 1991, 22.

66. *Al-Ahram*, January 3, 1992.

67. *Mideast Mirror*, January 3, 1992, 21-22.

68. *Mideast Mirror*, March 4, 1992, 18.

69. *Al-Hayat,* March 6, 1992, based on Western diplomats in Algiers.

70. According to the BBC news service.

71. Randal, *The Washington Post,* July 1, 1992, A26.

72. Jonathan C. Randal, "Crackdown in Algeria Slows Push by Radicals," *The Washington Post,* May 10, 1992, A30.

73. Ibid.

74. Boudiaf was assassinated by a counterintelligence officer in the Algerian armed forces. At the time of this writing, an investigation committee had been formed to look into the matter. Numerous reports have circulated that the assassination was planned by some state agencies alarmed by Boudiaf's uncompromising crusade against corruption in the state bureaucracy. Such claims were loudly and publicly expressed during Boudiaf's funeral. For more details on corruption in Algeria, see chapter 3, note 16.

Chapter 5

1. Morroe Berger, *The Arab World Today,* 170–71.

2. As cited in ibid., 171.

3. For more details, see Malcolm Kerr, *The Arab Cold War: Gamal Abd al-Nasir and His Rivals, 1958-1970* (Oxford: Oxford University Press, 1978 reprint).

4. More details about this phase are provided by Yezid Sayigh, "The Gulf Crisis: Why the Arab Regional Order Failed," *International Affairs 67,* no. 3 (1991): 490–92.

5. For more details about the key roles of these countries, see ibid., 494–97.

6. For example, Morocco, a longtime friend of the West that has maintained both secret and open relations with Israel, communicated to the United States and Western Europe the PLO position on a number of issues and mediated between the PLO and other Arab parties with which the organization was in conflict, such as Syria and Saudi Arabia. King Hasan has assumed a leadership role in an Islamic committee of heads of state entrusted with finding a peaceful resolution for the Arab-Israeli dispute over the city of Jerusalem. Algeria played a similar mediating role between the Palestinians and other parties, such as Syria and Libya, and until recently maintained good relations with Iran and revolutionary forces in the Third World, as well as with the West.

7. Tens of thousands of people took to the streets in Algeria, Morocco, Tunisia, Mauritania, and Libya chanting slogans against the Western military presence in the Gulf. Graffiti on street walls denounced the West and expressed strong support for Iraq.

8. "A Survey of the Middle East," *The Economist,* September 28, 1991, 6.

9. In the Gulf daily *al-Khaleej*, Ahmad al-Rab'i, a former Kuwaiti MP who was recently reelected, wrote about the anti-Arab xenophobia permeating Kuwait since the close of the Gulf War (*Mideast Mirror*, December 11, 1991, 21). In the Egyptian daily *al-Ahram*, the Egyptian commentator Salama Ahmad Salama accused the Kuwaiti authorities of creating a "climate of anti-Arab xenophobia" (*Mideast Mirror*, February 3, 1992, 11).

10. *Mideast Mirror*, February 3, 1992, 11.

11. *Mideast Mirror*, September 10, 1991, 16.

12. In a number of instances since the close of the war, the Arab League has revealed its weaknesses. One significant test was its failure to normalize relations between the anti-Saddam group and the rest of the Arab states, excluding Iraq. Another test was its dismal failure to settle the Libyan-Western conflict over the Lockerbie incident (see following note) before the UN Security Council decided on the embargo against Libya.

13. The UN Security Council passed a resolution in 1992 enforcing sanctions against Libya for failing to abide by an earlier resolution that ordered Libya to extradite two of its nationals for trial in the United States. The Libyans had been accused by a U.S. court of planting a bomb in 1988 on board a Pan Am flight. The bomb exploded over Lockerbie, Scotland, killing all passengers and crew as well as a number of people on the ground.

14. In apparent disbelief in the ability of both the GCC and Saudi Arabia to resolve its dispute with Bahrain over territorial waters and islands, Qatar sought arbitration by the International Court of Justice. Qatar has not withdrawn its request for international arbitration, despite Bahrain and Saudi Arabia's disapproval.

GCC countries have dealt with Iran in different ways. For instance, Qatar has signed an economic agreement with Iran, whereas the United Arab Emirates (U.A.E.) remains suspicious of Iranian designs after Iran took over all of Abu-Musa island. The security role of Iran in the Gulf, as well as the fate of the Damascus Declaration, remains a debatable subject among GCC states.

15. Sayigh, "The Gulf Crisis," 506.

16. Arab states and organizations that either disapproved, abstained, or were absent when voting on the Arab Summit's declaration on August 10, 1990, were the following: Iraq, Algeria, Libya, Tunisia, Jordan, Sudan, Yemen, and the PLO. Together, these countries or organizations represented over 104 million people out of a total of 235 million, or 44 percent of all Arabs.

17. A notable example is Morocco (with a population of 26 million), where pro-Iraq sentiments were obvious among people, parties, and demonstrators.

18. For further details, see chapter 2.

19. See Piscatori, "Religion and Realpolitik," 16.

20. At a private meeting with local journalists at his palace in Amman, King Hussein responded to the Saudi demand: "As I said from the outset of the crisis and I will always say, there is nothing for us to apologize for." (*Mideast Mirror*, April 3, 1992, 13).

21. Yousef Ibrahim of *The New York Times* (April 5, 1992) quotes an American diplomat as saying that the "individual interests of Arab states like Saudi Arabia, which needs American protection, and Egypt, which needs American money, transcend by far any notion of Arab solidarity." It may be noted that U.S. armed forces and advanced weaponry are still present in Saudi Arabia.

22. Syria appeared in both the 1992 and the 1993 lists published by the U.S. State Department of states that sponsor terrorism.

23. *Mideast Mirror*, March 12, 1992, 23, quoting Assad's speech to the People's Assembly in Damascus on March 12, 1992.

24. Syria's domain has, for some time, included parts of Lebanon— notably, the Bekaa, which borders both Israel and Syria. According to one interpretation of the Taef Accords, which initiated the recent domestic peace in Lebanon, Syrian forces, at the request of the Lebanese government, should have relocated to the Bekaa in September 1992.

25. *The Economist*, September 28, 1991, 9.

26. *Mideast Mirror*, September 18, 1991, 20, quoting *al-Ahali*, Cairo's opposition weekly.

27. Economic problems in Kuwait and Saudi Arabia as a result of the Gulf War are discussed in chapter 2.

28. See George Semaan, *al-Hayat*, May 10, 1992. Also cited in *Mideast Mirror*, May 11, 1992, 19–20.

29. *Mideast Mirror*, May 8, 1992, 14, quoting *Sawt al-Kuwait*.

30. *Mideast Mirror*, May 6, 1992, 11.

31. *Mideast Mirror*, September 16, 1991, 20.

32. *Mideast Mirror*, June 4, 1992, 22.

33. This contention is based on the published discussions among GCC representatives during their meetings between April 1991 and October 1992. See, for example, the Lebanese daily *al-Nahar*, September 10, 1992, 1 and 9.

34. *Mideast Mirror*, September 18, 1991, 19.

35. *Mideast Mirror*, October 28, 1991, 24.

36. *The Washington Post*, June 24, 1992, A23.

37. *Mideast Mirror*, June 23, 1992, 15.

38. See statement by Assistant Secretary of State Edward Djerejian to the House subcommittee on Europe and the Middle East, as quoted in *Mideast Mirror*, June 25, 1992, 13.

39. For further elaboration of the idea that unequal relationships of exchange produce resentment on the part of the beneficiary, see Peter Blau, *Exchange and Power in Social Life* (New York: Wiley, 1984).

40. See chapter 1 for details of the social and economic conditions in the Arab countries.

41. The Qatari government accused the Saudi armed forces of initiating the border clash, but the Saudi government denied the involvement of its troops. Instead, the Saudis described the incident as a clash between armed Bedouins and Qatari forces.

42. Border issues remain unresolved between each of the following couples of Arab states: Egypt and Sudan over the Halaib triangle, where Sudan gave a Canadian company an oil-exploration concession; Saudi Arabia and each of Iraq, the United Arab Emirates, Qatar, and Yemen; Kuwait and Iraq; Bahrain and Qatar; Oman and the United Arab Emirates; and Morocco and Mauritania over the Western Sahara, which also has involved Algeria in the past. At the time of this writing, some of these disputes were being negotiated (for example, the dispute between Oman and the United Arab Emirates) and are likely to be resolved amicably in the near future.

43. See Richard Schofield, "The Making of a Future War?," *al-Hayat*, as quoted by *Mideast Mirror*, April 6, 1992, 21.

44. In an op-ed piece in *The Washington Post* (August 2, 1992, C4) titled "Can the West Stop Saddam Before He Kills Iraq?," Nameer Ali Jawdat, a Washington, D.C., writer born in Baghdad, asserted that "most Iraqis, many Kuwaitis, and indeed most Arabs believe that Kuwait is an integral part of Iraq, artificially separated—and that the two will eventually reunite by common consent."

45. Caryle Murphy, "U.N. Map Makers Draw Kuwaiti-Iraqi Border," *The Washington Post*, May 5, 1992, A19–20.

46. Ibid.

47. From a statement by Ibrahim Burousli, chairman of the foreign affairs committee of Kuwait's National Council, as quoted in *Mideast Mirror*, May 1, 1992, 24.

48. *Mideast Mirror,* June 19, 1992, 19.

49. *Mideast Mirror*, May 28, 1992, 22.

50. President Saleh's interview was with *al-Quds al-Arabi* editor, as quoted in ibid., 23.

51. *Mideast Mirror*, May 29, 1992, 24; and June 1, 1992, 18.

52. *Mideast Mirror*, May 12, 1992, 18.

53. The Saudi spokesman said, "The Kingdom . . . has sought to negotiate with the Yemeni side about demarcating remaining parts of the border in line with the Taef Treaty, and has been concerned to achieve results that uphold the rights of both countries. But . . . found no serious desire on the Yemeni side to reach an agreement" (*Mideast Mirror,* May 29, 1992, 24).

54. Ibid.

55. *Mideast Mirror*, August 15, 1991, 14; November 18, 1991, 17; and April 22, 1992, 10.

56. *Mideast Mirror*, June 22, 1992, 15.

57. Qatar signed five economic agreements with Iran in late 1991, including one to construct a pipeline that pumps water from Iran to Qatar over 1,800 kilometers, costing an estimated $13 billion.

58. From Djerejian's statement to a congressional subcommittee, quoted in the *Mideast Mirror*, June 25, 1992, 11.

59. A good source on these water issues is John F. Kolars and William A. Mitchell, *The Euphrates River and the South East Anatolia Development Project* (Carbondale, Ill.: South Illinois University Press, 1991).

60. Other sources of potential conflict include bilateral disputes over borders, regional disputes over water resources, and failures to cooperate on such vital regional matters as arms proliferation and the status and movement of refugees and labor.

Chapter 6

1. *Mideast Mirror*, July 10, 1992, 21, quoting Ghazi al-Aridi's article in *al-Hayat*.

2. For example, on July 4, 1992, five policemen were killed after their two patrol cars were ambushed by gunmen. Later in July, after the Algerian military court sentenced the two FIS leaders Madani and Belhaj to 12 years in jail, their supporters demonstrated in a number of cities, clashing with the police. Five people were killed and about 100 arrested (*Mideast Mirror*, July 20, 1992, 20). Between July 1992 and January 1993, scores of people died in clashes between armed Islamists and the Algerian police.

3. For further details, see chapter 2 under "Egypt."

4. Roughly 1 million people are added to the Egyptian population every seven months.

5. This is in view of the generous rewards Egypt received from the West and the Gulf states and the Saudi provision of hundreds of thousands of work permits for Egyptians. For more details, see chapter 2.

6. These two points were discussed in chapter 3.

7. This point was discussed in chapter 3 under "Egypt."

8. For details, see Muhammad Faour, "Islam and Western Democracy: Opinion and Practice in the Contemporary Middle East" (Paper delivered at the United States Institute of Peace symposium on Islam and Democracy, Washington, D.C., May 15, 1992).

9. Pope Shenouda, head of the Coptic Christian church, told a press conference that the Christians of Assyut were attacked by Islamic fundamentalists because of their religion rather than "vendettas" and that they needed more protection from the state. He also said that the Egyptian government had been hindering the construction of new churches (*Mideast Mirror*, July 7, 1992, 20). For more details about the Copts' appeals to Western leaders, see chapter 4.

10. For details about the serious inaccuracy of U.S. intelligence information, see the U.S. News and World Report book, *Triumph Without Victory: The Unreported History of the Persian Gulf War* (New York: Times Books, 1992).

11. This is the substance of a well-known sociological proposition first advanced by Georg Simmel and later reformulated by Lewis Coser. See Georg Simmel, *Conflict*, Kurt H. Wolff, trans. (Glencoe, Ill.: The Free Press, 1955); and Lewis A. Coser, *The Functions of Social Conflict* (Glencoe, Ill.: The Free Press, 1956), chapter V.

12. Roberts, "A Trial of Strength," 143.

13. For more details of the results of the Kuwaiti elections, see *al-Hayat*, October 8, 1992, 7.

14. For more details, see chapter 2.

15. This was reaffirmed in unequivocal terms by Assistant Secretary of State Djerejian in a statement to the House. For his full statement, see *Mideast Mirror*, June 25, 1992, 11.

16. The decline of pan-Arabism is discussed in chapter 4.

17. Domestic destabilizers are discussed in the previous section of this chapter, and external, regional destabilizers are discussed in chapter 5.

18. One of the lessons learned from the history of the Arab-Israeli conflict is that "negotiations have only succeeded at moments when the status quo seemed more painful or dangerous than a potential negotiated compromise, at least for some of the parties" (United States Institute of Peace, *Making Peace Among Arabs and Israelis: Lessons from Fifty Years of Experience* [Washington, D.C.: United States Institute of Peace, 1992], 14).

19. This point is elaborated in chapter 5.

20. *Mideast Mirror*, November 19, 1991, 2–4.

21. *Mideast Mirror*, December 12, 1991, 10–14.

22. See, for example, an article in the *Jerusalem Post* quoted in *Mideast Mirror*, July 17, 1992, 9.

23. The United Nations provides the following geographic distribution of Palestinian "refugees": 274,000 in Syria, 294,000 in Lebanon, 900,000 in Jordan, 398,000 in the West Bank, and 469,000 in Gaza.

24. See Assad's interview with Patrick Seale, *al-Wasat*, no. 67 (May 10–16, 1993): 12–20. If an Arab party "gives up Arab rights," said Assad, "we will oppose it." And when an Arab party is close to an agreement with Israel, "we will study whether some participants should sign bilateral accords, and whether or not that will serve the collective interest."

25. This option was suggested by George Jukman, a Palestinian philosophy professor at Bir Zeit University, in an op-ed piece in *al-Hayat*, May 21, 1992.

26. In an attempt to design such a formula, former Secretary of State Henry Kissinger suggested that Israel grant "genuine self-government to the largest possible area of the West Bank in keeping with reasonable security objectives" but postpone discussion of final frontiers and the future of Jerusalem until the would-be interim agreement has passed the test of time (Henry Kissinger, "The Path to Successful Coexistence in the Middle East," *The Washington Post*, August 2, 1992, C7).

27. For details, see the Economist Intelligence Unit, *Syria, Country Report*, no. 2 (1992).

28. This view with regard to an interim agreement with Syria concurs with that of Henry Kissinger, who also thinks that President Assad is likely to prefer some territorial adjustment in the Golan Heights "to a formal peace agreement, which in any event he will only conclude after the Palestinian issue is finally resolved" (Kissinger, "The Path to Successful Coexistence").

29. See note 18, chapter 6.

Sources Used

Newspapers and Magazines

The following Arabic papers and magazines were monitored from September 1, 1991, through August 1, 1992:

al-Ahram (Egyptian daily)
Ashsharq-al-Awsat (Saudi daily)
al-Hawadeth (Lebanese, pan-Arab weekly)
al-Hayat (Lebanese, pan-Arab daily)
al-Jazira al-Arabiyya (Saudi opposition-in-exile monthly)
al-Wasat (Lebanese, pan-Arab weekly)
Sawt al-Kuwait (Kuwaiti daily)

Between August 1992 and January 1993, three were monitored:

Ash-shiraa (Lebanese weekly)
al-Hayat
al-Nahar (Lebanese daily)

The following English-language newspapers and magazines were monitored during the periods indicated:

The Economist, September 1990–September 1991.
Middle East International, January 1992–August 1992.
Middle East Report, July/August 1991–July/August 1992.
Mideast Mirror, November 1990–July 1992.
Newsweek, August 1990–January 1993.
The New York Times, September 1990–July 1992.
Time, August 1990–January 1993.
The Washington Post, September 1991–August 1992.

Books, Reports, and Journal Articles

al-Mawdudi, Abul A'la. *Islamic Way of Life*, 11th ed. Lahore, Pakistan: Islamic Publications, 1979.

al-Wardi, Ali. *Shakhsiyyat al-Fard al-'Iraqi* (The personality of the Iraqi individual). Baghdad: al-Rabita Press, 1951.

Ansari, Hamid. *Egypt: The Stalled Society*. Albany, N.Y.: State University of New York Press, 1986.

Aristotle. *The Politics of Aristotle*, E. Barker, trans. Oxford: Clarendon, 1961.

Ayubi, Nazih N. "Domestic Politics." In Lilian C. Harris, ed., *Egypt: Internal Challenges and Regional Stability*. New York: Routledge and Kegan Paul, 1988.

Baram, Amatzia. "Territorial Nationalism in the Middle East." *Middle Eastern Studies* (London) 26, no. 4 (October 1990).

Batatu, Hanna. "Political Power and Social Structure in Syria and Iraq." In Samih Farsoun, ed., *Arab Society: Continuity and Change*, 34–37. London: Croom Helm, 1985.

Berger, Morroe. *The Arab World Today*. New York: Doubleday & Company, Inc., 1962.

Binder, Leonard. *In a Moment of Enthusiasm: Political Power and the Second Stratum*. Chicago: University of Chicago Press, 1978.

Binder, Leonard. *Islamic Liberalism: A Critique of Development Ideologies*. Chicago: Chicago University Press, 1989.

Blau, Peter. *Exchange and Power in Social Life*. New York: Wiley, 1984.

Blaustein, Albert P., and Gilbert H. Flanz, eds. *Constitutions of the Countries of the World*. New York: Oceana Publications, 1990.

Coser, Lewis A. *The Functions of Social Conflict*. Glencoe, Ill.: The Free Press, 1956.

Dahl, Robert A. *Democracy and Its Critics*. New Haven, Conn., and London: Yale University Press, 1989.

Dahl, Robert A. *Polyarchy: Participation and Opposition*. New Haven, Conn., and London: Yale University Press, 1971.

The Economist Intelligence Unit. *Country Reports* for 1992 and no. 1, 1993, and *Country Profiles* for 1992–93 for *Iraq, Jordan, Kuwait, Saudi Arabia, and Syria*. London: The Economist Intelligence Unit.

Esposito, John L., and James P. Piscatori. "Democratization and Islam." *Middle East Journal* 45, no. 3 (1991).

Europa Publications. *The Europa World Year Book 1991*. London: Europa Publications.

Europa Publications, *The Middle East and North Africa 1992*. London: Europa Publications, 1992.

Faour, Muhammad. "Democracy and the Arab World: A Study of Four Countries." In Elise Boulding, ed., *The Middle East in the Twenty-First Century: Scenarios for Peace Building*. Forthcoming.

Fisher, Sydney N., and William Ochsenwald. *The Middle East: A History*, 4th ed. New York: McGraw-Hill, Inc., 1990.

Foreign Broadcasting Information Service Daily Report: Near East and South Asia. Monitored between October 1991 and July 1992.

Gastil, Raymond D. *Freedom in the World: Political Rights and Civil Liberties, 1990–1991.* New York: Freedom House, 1991.

Ghabra, Shafiq. "The Iraqi Occupation of Kuwait: An Eyewitness Account." *Journal of Palestine Studies* 20, no. 2 (Winter 1991).

Giddens, Anthony. *The Nation-State and Violence.* Berkeley, Calif.: University of California Press, 1987.

Gurr, Ted R., Keith Jaggers, and Will H. Moore. *Polity II Handbook.* Boulder, Colo.: University of Colorado, 1989.

Harik, Iliya. "The Origins of the Arab State System." In Ghassan Salamé, ed., *The Foundations of the Arab State.* London: Croom Helm, 1987.

Herodotus. *The Histories*, A. de Selincourt, trans., rev. ed. Middlesex, England: Penguin, 1984.

Hiro, Dilip. *The Longest War: The Iran-Iraq Military Conflict.* New York: Routledge, 1991.

Hourani, Albert. *A History of the Arab Peoples.* Cambridge, Mass.: Harvard University Press, 1991.

Hourani, Albert. *Syria and Lebanon.* London: Oxford University Press, 1946.

Hudson, Michael C. "After the Gulf War: Prospects for Democratization in the Arab World." *Middle East Journal* 45, no. 3 (1991).

Huntington, Samuel P. "How Countries Democratize." *Political Science Quarterly* 106, no. 4 (Winter 1991–92).

Huntington, Samuel P. "Will More Countries Become Democratic?" In Samuel Huntington and Joseph Nye, Jr., eds., *Global Dilemmas*, 253–79. Cambridge, Mass.: Harvard University Press, 1985.

Ismael, Tareq, and Jacqueline Ismael. "The Legacy of Nationalism." In Tareq Ismael and Jacqueline Ismael, eds., *Politics and Government in the Middle East and North Africa.* Miami: Florida International University Press, 1991.

Jadaane, Fahmi. "Notions of the State in Contemporary Arab-Islamic Writings." In Ghassan Salamé, ed., *The Foundations of the Arab State*, 112–48. London: Croom Helm, 1987.

Keddourie, Elie. *In the Anglo-Arab Labyrinth: The McMahon-Husayn Correspondence and Its Interpretations, 1914–1939.* Cambridge, England: Cambridge University Press, 1976.

Kerr, Malcolm. *The Arab Cold War: Gamal Abd al-Nasir and His Rivals, 1958-1970.* Oxford: Oxford University Press, 1978 reprint.

Kolars, John F., and William A. Mitchell. *The Euphrates River and the South East Anatolia Development Project.* Carbondale, Ill.: South Illinois University Press, 1991.

Laipson, Ellen, and Alfred Prados. *Jordan: Recent Developments and Implications for U.S. Interests.* CRS Report for Congress, July 11, 1990.

Luciani, Giacomo, and Hazem Beblawi. *The Rentier State.* London: Croom Helm, 1987.

Middle East Watch. *Empty Reforms: Saudi Arabia's New Basic Laws.* New York: Human Rights Watch, May 1992.

Middle East Watch. "Kuwait: Deteriorating Human Rights Conditions Since the Early Occupation." *News from the Middle East,* November 19, 1990.

Middle East Watch. *A Victory Turned Sour: Human Rights in Kuwait Since Liberation.* New York: Human Rights Watch, September 1991.

Milton-Edwards, Beverley. "A Temporary Alliance with the Crown: The Islamic Response in Jordan." In James Piscatori, ed., *Islamic Fundamentalisms and the Gulf Crisis.* Chicago: Academy of Arts and Sciences, 1992.

Minority Rights Group, ed. *World Directory of Minorities.* Essex, England: Longman International Reference, 1990.

Piscatori, James. "Religion and Realpolitik: Islamic Responses to the Gulf War." In James Piscatori, ed., *Islamic Fundamentalisms and the Gulf Crisis.* Chicago: Academy of Arts and Sciences, 1992.

Roberts, Hugh. "A Trial of Strength: Algerian Islamism." In James Piscatori, ed., *Islamic Fundamentalisms and the Gulf Crisis.* Chicago: Academy of Arts and Sciences, 1992.

Rothstein, Robert L. "Democracy, Conflict, and Development in the Third World." *Washington Quarterly* (Spring 1991).

Rummel, Rudolph. "Libertarianism and International Violence." *Journal of Conflict Resolution,* no. 27 (March 1983): 27–71.

Sartori, Giovanni. *Democratic Theory.* New York: Praeger, 1965.

Sayigh, Yezid. "The Gulf Crisis: Why the Arab Regional Order Failed." *International Affairs* 67, no. 3 (1991).

Schmitter, Philippe. "Society." In National Research Council, *The Transition to Democracy: Proceedings of a Workshop.* Washington, D.C.: National Academy Press, 1991.

Sharabi, Hisham. "The Dialectics of Patriarchy in Arab Society." In Samih Farsoun, ed., *Arab Society: Continuity and Change,* 83–104. London: Croom Helm, 1985.

Simmel, Georg. *Conflict.* Kurt H. Wolff, trans. Glencoe, Ill.: The Free Press, 1955.

Taylor, Alan. *The Arab Balance of Power System.* Syracuse, N.Y.: Syracuse University Press, 1982.

Tibi, Bassam. "The Simultaneity of the Unsimultaneous: Old Tribes and Imposed Nation-States in the Modern Middle East." In Philip Khoury and Joseph Kostiner, eds., *Tribes and State Formation in the Middle East,* 127–52. Berkeley, Calif.: University of California Press, 1990.

United Nations High Commissioner for Refugees. All *Information Bulletins* issued on Iraq between September 1991 and February 1992.

United States Institute of Peace. *Making Peace Among Arabs and Israelis: Lessons from Fifty Years of Experience.* Washington, D.C.: United States Institute of Peace, 1992.

U.S. News and World Report. *Triumph Without Victory: The Unreported History of the Persian Gulf War.* New York: Times Books, 1992.

Viorst, Milton. "A Reporter at Large: After the Liberation." *New Yorker,* September 30, 1991, 37–72.

Unpublished Papers and Manuscripts

Barnett, Michael N. "Sovereignty, Institutions, and Identity: From Pan-Arabism to the Arab State System." Paper delivered at the 1991 Annual Meeting of the American Political Science Association, Washington, D.C., August 29–September 1, 1991.

Batatu, Hanna. "The Egyptian, Syrian and Iraqi Revolutions: Some Observations on Their Underlying Causes and Social Character." Inaugural lecture given at Center for Contemporary Arab Studies, Georgetown University, January 25, 1983.

Brown, Carl. "Patterns Forged in Time: Middle Eastern Mindsets and the Gulf War." Paper delivered at the Conference on the Political Psychology of the Gulf War: Leaders, Publics and the Process of Conflict, City University of New York, November 11–12, 1991.

Faour, Muhammad. "Islam and Western Democracy: Opinion and Practice in the Contemporary Middle East." Paper delivered at the United States Institute of Peace symposium on Islam and Democracy, Washington, D.C., May 15, 1992.

Gause, F. Gregory. "Sovereignty, Statecraft and Stability in the Middle East." Paper delivered at the Annual Meeting of the American Political Science Association, Washington, D.C., August 29–September 1, 1984.

George, Alexander. "The Gulf War: Possible Impact on the International System." Paper presented at the Conference on the Political Psychology of the Gulf War: Leaders, Publics and the Process of Conflict, City University of New York, November 11–12, 1991.

Maoz, Zeev, and Bruce Russett. "Alliances, Contiguity, Wealth, and Political Stability: Is the Lack of Conflict among Democracies a Statistical Artifact?" Paper delivered at the Annual Meeting of the American Political Science Association, San Francisco, August 30–September 2, 1990.

Offen, Elizabeth N. "The Persian Gulf War of 1990/1991: Its Impact on Migration and the Security of States." Unpublished manuscript, Department of Political Science, MIT, December 1991.

Oweiss, Ibrahim M. "Economic Impact of the Gulf War with Special Reference to the Economies of Selected Arab Countries." Unpublished manuscript, Georgetown University, 1992.

Owdeh, Adnan Abu. Talk at the United States Institute of Peace symposium on Islam and Democracy, Washington, D.C., May 15, 1992.

Personal Interviews

The following people were interviewed by the author between July 1991 and July 1992:

Barakat, Halim. Professor of Sociology, Center for Contemporary Arab Studies, Georgetown University.

Batatu, Hanna. Professor of Political Science, Center for Contemporary Arab Studies, Georgetown University.

Daouk, Muhammad Amin. Lawyer and president of the Islamic Center, Beirut, Lebanon.

Farsoun, Samih. Professor of Sociology, American University.

George, Alexander. Graham H. Stuart Professor of International Relations, Stanford University.

Khalil, Mohamed Ibrahim. Lawyer who has held a number of important academic and government positions in Sudan, including that of speaker of the Sudanese Constitutional Assembly, minister of foreign affairs, minister of justice, and dean of the Faculty of Law and Shari'a at Khartoum University.

Milhem, Hisham. Journalist in Washington, D.C., and correspondent for Radio Monte Carlo and the Lebanese daily *Assafir*.

Oweiss, Ibrahim. Professor of Economics, Center for Contemporary Arab Studies, Georgetown University.

Peretz, Don. Professor of Political Science, State University of New York, Binghamton.

Rayyan, Abdullatif. Journalist in Washington, D.C., and correspondent for the Jerusalem daily *al-Quds*.

Rothstein, Robert. Harvey Picker Distinguished Professor of International Relations, Colgate University.

Sammak, Muhammad. Writer and adviser to a number of Lebanese political and religious leaders, Beirut, Lebanon.

Sharabi, Hisham. Professor of History and Government, Center for Contemporary Arab Studies, Georgetown University.

Index

United States Institute of Peace

The United States Institute of Peace is an independent, nonpartisan federal institution created and funded by Congress to strengthen the nation's capacity to promote the peaceful resolution of international conflict. Established in 1984, the Institute meets its congressional mandate through an array of programs, including grants, fellowships, conferences and workshops, library services, publications and other educational activities. The Institute's Board of Directors is appointed by the President of the United States and confirmed by the Senate.

Jennings Randolph Program for International Peace

As part of the statute establishing the United States Institute of Peace, Congress envisioned a fellowship program that would appoint "scholars and leaders of peace from the United States and abroad to pursue scholarly inquiry and other appropriate forms of communication on international peace and conflict resolution." The program was named after Senator Jennings Randolph of West Virginia, whose efforts over four decades helped to establish the Institute.

Since it began in 1987, the Jennings Randolph Program has played a key role in the Institute's effort to build a national center of research, dialogue, and education on critical problems of conflict and peace. Through a rigorous annual competition, outstanding men and women from diverse nations and fields are selected to carry out projects designed to expand and disseminate knowledge on violent international conflict and the wide range of ways it can be peacefully managed or resolved.

The Institute's Distinguished Fellows and Peace Fellows are individuals from a wide variety of academic and other professional backgrounds who work at the Institute on research and education projects they have proposed and participate in the Institute's collegial and public outreach activities. The Institute's Peace Scholars are doctoral candidates at American universities who are working on their dissertations.

Institute fellows and scholars have worked on such varied subjects as international negotiation, regional security arrangements, conflict resolution techniques, international legal systems, ethnic and religious conflict, arms control, and the protection of human rights, and these issues have been examined in settings throughout the world.

As part of its effort to disseminate original and useful analyses of peace and conflict to policymakers and the public, the Institute publishes book manuscripts and other written products that result from the fellowship work and meet the Institute's high standards of quality.

Michael S. Lund
Director

ॐ

THE ARAB WORLD
AFTER DESERT STORM

The text of this book is set in Poppl Pontifex; the display type is Albertus.

Cover design by Laurie Rosenthal of Meadows and Wiser; interior design by Joan Engelhardt and Day Wilkes; map prepared by Marie Marr-Williams. Page makeup by Helene Y. Redmond of HYR Graphics. Editorial work by Jill Shepherd of EEI, Paula Bailey-Smith, Dan Snodderly, and Nigel Quinney.